HEALING A SPOUSE'S
GRIEVING HEART

Also by Alan Wolfelt:

Creating Meaningful Funeral Ceremonies:
A Guide for Families

Healing a Child's Grieving Heart:
100 Practical Ideas for Families, Friends
and Caregivers

Healing a Friend's Grieving Heart:
100 Practical Ideas for Helping Someone
You Love Through Loss

Healing a Teen's Grieving Heart:
100 Practical Ideas for Families, Friends
and Caregivers

Healing Your Grieving Heart for Kids:
100 Practical Ideas

The Journey Through Grief:
Reflections on Healing

Understanding Your Grief: Ten Essential
Touchstones For Finding Hope
and Healing Your Heart

Companion Press is dedicated to the education and support of both the bereaved and bereavement caregivers.

We believe that those who companion the bereaved by walking with them as they journey in grief have a wondrous opportunity: to help others embrace and grow through grief—and to lead fuller, more deeply-lived lives themselves because of this important ministry.

Companion
P R E S S

For a complete catalog and
ordering information, write or call:

Companion Press
The Center for Loss and Life Transition
3735 Broken Bow Road
Fort Collins, CO 80526
(970) 226-6050
www.centerforloss.com

HEALING A SPOUSE'S GRIEVING HEART

•

100 PRACTICAL IDEAS AFTER YOUR HUSBAND OR WIFE DIES

Compassionate advice and simple activities for widows and widowers

•

ALAN D. WOLFELT, PH.D.

Companion
P R E S S

Fort Collins, Colorado
An imprint of the Center for Loss and Life Transition

Companion Press is an imprint of the
Center for Loss and Life Transition,
3735 Broken Bow Road, Fort Collins, Colorado 80526

Companion Press books may be purchased in bulk for sales promotions, premiums or fundraisers. Please contact the publisher at the above address for more information.

Printed in the United States of America

18 17 16 15 14   8 7 6

ISBN: 978-1-879651-37-1

*In loving memory of the soulmate relationship of my
Aunt Helen and Uncle Bob, and in gratitude for the
model they provided for a loving relationship with
another human being.
Helen and Bob Mansfield were married
on December 26, 1943.*

*Helen died on July 28, 2001.
This couple loved each other deeply and with
passion. To them I dedicate this book.*

"Bereavement is a universal and integral part of our experience of love. It follows marriage as normally as marriage follows courtship or as autumn follows summer. It is not a truncation of the process but one of the phases; not the interruption of the dance, but the next figure. We are taken out of ourselves by the loved one when he is here. Then comes the tragic figure dance in which we must learn to be taken out of ourselves though the bodily presence is withdrawn."

C.S. Lewis, *A Grief Observed*

CONTENTS

INTRODUCTION

"Until death do us part."

Many of us stood before our family and friends and made this promise to our new spouses. We committed to love, honor, and cherish, for richer or poorer, in sickness and in health. We believed in the power of love to conquer all things. Of course, at the time, most of us had no concept of the formidable foe that is sickness or the unbreachable chasm that is death.

As intrepid travelers on the journey into loving and being loved by another person, we open ourselves to all that may happen along the way. We join in a shared union and experience the ups and downs that come with the sweetness (and the normal occasional bitterness!) of the connection.

If we are fortunate, as our relationships evolve we become increasingly comfortable meeting each other in the richness of our humanity—sharing our strengths and our weaknesses, our joys and our sorrows. A vital part of loving well means accepting those we love, their gifts as well as their flaws.

Even in the face of all the mysteries of life, it is so grounding to know there is another person who catches our spirit. It may be as simple as the way she walks or the sparkle in her eyes. Something connects you in a way that makes both of you feel alive. There is a change from *me* to *us* and a shared commitment to live life together with mutual meaning and purpose. Love has given us faith in each other and in the world. We feel safer, almost immortal.

I believe that loving another person is one of the ways we reach out to God. Shared love answers our need for meaning, adventure, and connection to another human being. Authentic love is a miracle and we have touched it.

Yet, even surrounded by our faith and love, inevitable loss lurks in the background. When that special person we love dies, we are broken in ways never imagined. Despite the certainty that death will enter into our lives, most of us are unprepared for it.

We feel torn from the familiar, as if our world has been turned upside down. Our everyday lives have come apart, shattered in myriad ways. We may fear that we cannot be ourselves in a world forever changed by this profound loss, that investing ourselves in life and living again will no longer bring us happiness and joy.

You are beginning, or are in the midst of, a journey that is frightening, painful, and sometimes lonely. No words, written or spoken, can take away the pain you feel now. I am truly sorry that your spouse has died. As a grief counselor and educator, and as a man who has been married to my wife, Sue, for 18 years, I have the deepest empathy for you. In my frequent travels across North America, speaking and teaching about grief, I have had the privilege to meet hundreds and hundreds of widows. They come to me with their stories of loss—and, ultimately, healing—and I bear witness and learn from them.

I pass their messages of hope and healing on to you now. They want you know that you will survive, though if you are early in your grief, you may find this hard to believe. The death of a spouse tears through every layer of your existence. It will take time and hard work to sew up those many tears, and even then the "repairs" will always be a part of who you are. Healing does not mean forgetting or "getting over."

In fact, there is no such thing as "getting over" grief. That term is the cruelest of fallacies. You don't "get over" grief. You learn to live with it. You learn to accommodate it and make it part of who you are. But if you mourn well, over time and with the support of others, your grief will soften. No, it will never end, and it is likely that a day won't go by that you don't think about and miss your precious husband or wife. But, your grief will become less sharp and all-consuming. It will take on the blurred, bittersweet qualities of memory. On most days, it will murmur gently in the background while in the foreground, your life proceeds with meaning and purpose.

Older adult widows: Mourn!

Sometimes people think that just because you were married a long time and your spouse was "old" when he died, you shouldn't mourn his death. After all, the reasoning goes, you were lucky to have him as long as you did and it's a fact of life that people do die when they get older. Besides, almost half of all women 65 years old and older are widows. Widowhood is so common in old age that you shouldn't complain.

Poppycock! You grieve and so you must mourn! Your precious partner of many, many years is gone. Your whole life may have been built around this person and now that she's gone, your whole life has been torn apart. Of course you're in shock. Of course you're sad. Of course you're unsure how or if you'll survive.

My own mother and father were high school sweethearts and proudly celebrated their 50th wedding anniversary in July of 1999. Four months later, my father died from malignant melanoma. My mother was, and is, bereaved—which literally means to be torn apart and to have special needs.

As I write these words, it has been three and a half years since I became a grieving son and my mother a "widow." She has been told by many people, "Well, you had him 50 years. Be thankful!" She is indeed thankful. But like many of you, she would have liked to have had him for another 50.

Life is different without her best friend, her confidant, her life partner. Like you, she has been faced with the need to mourn openly and authentically. Yes, mourn! Express your grief outside yourself. Talk to your friends about the death. Talk to your children. Write about it in a journal. Paint it. Take up a cause in your spouse's honor. Create a marital memory book of photos and memorabilia. Pray.

If you actively mourn your beloved spouse's death, you will not only come to live the rest of your own life more happily and more fully, you will also be actively honoring and remembering your marriage. And you will grow to learn that you can mourn and live at the same time. Your life without your spouse can also be rich and satisfying, if always a little bittersweet. This book is my invitation to you to join my mother and thousands of other widows who each day confront the need to re-discover a reason to get their feet out of bed when their lifeline has been severed.

Young widows take heart

In my grief workshops across North America, I have had the privilege to meet and get to know many young widows and widowers. Perhaps like you, they are often shocked and often angry that their lifetime partners were taken from them so very early! You have every right to be shocked and angry. You built your life on what you thought was a solid foundation, only to have that foundation crack and crumble.

If you find yourself floundering, know that this is a common experience for the half a million Americans widowed under the age of 45. Many have young children and young careers, both of which demand lots of attention. Many struggle financially on one income. Many cannot decide if or when they should date again.

There are no rules to young widowhood. You must do what feels right for you. You must forge your own path. Talking to other young widows, either informally or in the safety net of a support group, may help you find your way. And the young widows I have met would want me to tell you that somehow, some way, not only will you survive, you will learn to live and love again.

A note for gay mourners

Of course, when your partner dies, your loss is as real and as devastating as that of a heterosexual spouse's. Not being married in the eyes of the law doesn't make the love—or the subsequent pain—any less true. But your sexual orientation may in fact "disenfranchise" your grief. Why? Because if society is unaccepting of your love, they will be equally unaccepting of your grief. Your loss cannot be sanctioned if your love was not sanctioned. Legal, probate, and family issues can also complicate matters for gay widows. I hope you have a circle of close friends and family who supported your relationship with your partner and who will be supportive of your need to mourn. If not, perhaps you can find an appropriate support group, either in person or online.

Finally, I use the term "spouse" throughout this book not to disenfranchise your experience but for ease of reference. You may be interested to know that the word "spouse" comes from the Old French for "to pledge." If you pledged your love and your commitment to your partner, whether legally or spiritually, you, too, were a "spouse."

An invitation to mourn

Whether your spouse was young when he or she died or elderly, whether the death was the result of an illness, an accident, a homicide, or suicide, whether the death was sudden or lingering, the messages I am honored to bring you in this book are for you. There are 100 of them, and some will speak to your experience more precisely than others. If you come to an idea that doesn't seem to fit you, simply ignore it and turn to another page.

Some of the 100 ideas will teach you about the principles of grief and mourning. One of the most important ways to help yourself is to learn about the grief experience. The remainder of the 100 ideas offer practical, here-and-now, action-oriented suggestions for embracing your grief and practicing self-compassion. Each idea is followed by a brief explanation of how and why the idea might help you.

You'll also notice that each of the 100 ideas offers a "carpe diem," which means "seize the day." My hope is that you not relegate this book to your shelves but instead keep it handy on your nightstand or desk.

Pick it up often and turn to any page; the carpe diem suggestion might help you seize the day by giving you an exercise, action, or thought to consider today, right now, right this minute.

Please note that to make the language less cumbersome I am using the term "widow" throughout this text to encompass both widows and widowers. When I say "widow" I make no gender distinction and I mean for my suggestions to apply equally to both men and women. You may also notice that I alternate gender pronouns, sometimes using "he" and sometimes "she." I do this simply to avoid having to say "he or she" every time.

While I do not believe in ranking losses in an attempt to define which kinds of losses are most painful and devastating to survivors, I have learned that widows have a particularly difficult journey ahead of them. Counselors sometimes rate the death of a spouse as the greatest stress in life.

But remember, you are not alone and your struggles are not forgotten. Each year more than a million Americans become widows, joining the more than 12 million already in existence. They want you to know that you can not only learn to survive but go on to discover renewal of meaning and purpose in your life. I am honored to pass along these resounding messages of hope and healing to you.

I thank you from deep in my soul for having the courage to embrace the thoughts I've tried to express in this book. I hope we meet one day!

Alan D. Wolfelt

1.
UNDERSTAND THE DIFFERENCE BETWEEN GRIEF AND MOURNING

- Grief is what we think and feel on the inside when someone we love dies.

- Mourning is the outward expression of our grief.

- Everyone grieves when someone loved dies, but if we are to heal, we must also mourn.

- Many of the ideas in this book are intended to help you mourn the death of your spouse—to express your grief outside of yourself. Over time and with the support of others, to mourn is to heal.

- Mourning the death of a spouse isn't always easy. As a culture, we tend to be uncomfortable with outward expressions of grief. We sometimes feel ashamed or weak if we show our innermost feelings. Yet the truth is, it takes strength and perseverance to mourn.

- If some of your friends and family are not compassionately supporting your need to mourn, seek out the company of those who will.

CARPE DIEM:
Ask yourself this: Have I been mourning my spouse's death or have I restricted myself to grieving?

2.
KNOW THAT YOU ARE NOT ALONE

- Your relationship with your spouse was unique. Your grief is unique, too. No other widow or widower will grieve in exactly the same way. No one else will have precisely the same thoughts and feelings.

- Still, you are not alone. Millions of others have experienced the death of a spouse in the last five years. Millions more will lose a partner in the coming decade. According to the Census Bureau, at any given time about 12% of the U.S. population has been widowed—2% of all men and 10% of all women. And this number does not include deaths among same sex partners and unmarried heterosexual couples.

- Some people like to point out that widowhood happens to half of all married people. This is not to say that something is simple or unimportant just because it is commonplace. On the contrary, the loss of a partner is among life's most wrenching and challenging experiences.

- Many others before you have walked the path that you now walk. They are all around you—in your neighborhood, your workplace, your community groups, your place of worship. And many of them would like to offer you the support that only another widow can. Open up to others and in turn they will open up to you.

CARPE DIEM:
Think about whom you know who has also lost a spouse or partner. Make an effort to spend some time talking with one of these people today.

3.
BE COMPASSIONATE
WITH YOURSELF

- The journey through grief is a long and difficult one. It is also a journey for which there is no preparation.

- You have lost your life partner, perhaps your soulmate and best friend. The person who may have known you better than anyone else is now gone. To feel lonely, angry, deeply sad, and other difficult emotions is not only normal, it is necessary.

- Be compassionate with yourself as you encounter these painful thoughts and feelings.

- Don't judge yourself or try to set a particular course for healing. There is no one way to grieve the death of a spouse. There is only what you think and feel and the expressing of those thoughts and feelings.

- Let your journey be what it is. And let yourself—your new, grieving self—be who you are.

CARPE DIEM:
If you have the energy, take a walk today through a quiet area of town. Or better yet, get out of town and find a "safe place" in nature. Rest when you're tired and contemplate the ways in which you might take better care of yourself in the coming weeks and months.

4.
ACKNOWLEDGE THE UNIQUENESS OF YOUR WIDOWHOOD

- Your unique grief journey will be shaped by many factors, including:
  - the nature of the relationship you had with your husband or wife.
  - the age of the spouse who died as well as your own age.
  - how long you were married.
  - the circumstances of the death.
  - your family's coping and communication styles.
  - your unique personality.
  - your cultural background.
  - your religious or spiritual beliefs.
  - your gender.
  - your support systems.

- Because of these and other factors, no two deaths are ever mourned in precisely the same way. If other people in your life have died, you may find that this grief feels similar or completely different.

- If you are a younger widow, your circumstances and needs will probably be very different than if you're an older widow—and vice versa. Financial matters, social issues, remarriage, childcare—all these things can be markedly different depending upon your age.

- Don't have rigid expectations for your thoughts, feelings, and behaviors. Instead, accept and even celebrate your uniqueness.

CARPE DIEM:

Reach out to get your unique mourning needs met today. Find someone close to your age and circumstances who is also a widow—someone who can truly affirm and honor the power of your story.

5.
ALLOW FOR NUMBNESS

- Feelings of shock, numbness, and disbelief are nature's way of temporarily protecting us from the full reality of the death of someone loved. They help us survive our early grief. Thank God for numbness and denial.

- We often think, "I will wake up and this will not have happened." Mourning can feel like being in a dream. The world feels distant, almost unreal—especially the lives of other people. The world turns but you may not feel it. Time elapses, but you may not experience it.

- Your emotions need time to catch up with what your mind has been told. This is true even when death has followed a long illness.

- Even after you have moved beyond your initial feelings of shock, numbness, and disbelief, don't be surprised if they resurface. Birthdays, holidays and anniversaries, and other special occasions often trigger these normal and necessary feelings.

- You may want to reach out and let others you trust know when you are experiencing waves of numbness and disbelief. Their compassionate support will help you through these difficult times.

CARPE DIEM:
If you're feeling numb, cancel any commitments that require concentration and decision-making. Allow yourself time to regroup.

6.
EXPECT TO HAVE A MULTITUDE OF FEELINGS

- Mourners don't just feel sad. We may feel numb, angry, guilty, afraid, confused, or even relieved. Sometimes these feelings follow each other within a short period of time or they may occur simultaneously.

- As strange as some of these emotions may seem to you, they are normal and healthy.

- Think of your feelings as friends to be understood, not enemies to be fought. In part, the function of your feelings is to remind you that you have "special needs." Your task is to pay attention to your unique special needs.

- Allow yourself to feel whatever it is you are feeling without judging yourself.

- Talk about your feelings with someone who cares and can supportively listen.

CARPE DIEM:

Which emotion has surprised you most since your spouse's death? In your mind, single out this emotion for a moment and give it play. Embrace it. Honor it. And affirm it by talking to someone else who has journeyed through grief after the death of a spouse.

7.

BE AWARE THAT YOUR GRIEF AFFECTS YOUR BODY, HEART, MIND, SOCIAL SELF, AND SPIRIT

- Grief is physically demanding. The body responds to the stress of the encounter and the immune system can weaken. You may be more susceptible to illness and physical discomforts. You may also feel lethargic or highly fatigued. (We call this the "lethargy of grief.") You may not be sleeping well.

- The emotional toll of grief is complex and painful. Mourners often feel many different feelings, and those feelings can shift and blur over time.

- Cognitive disorientation is common in grief. You may find yourself unable to think clearly, stay on task, or remember everyday things.

- Bereavement naturally results in social discomfort. Friends and family often withdraw from mourners, leaving us isolated and unsupported. While I hope this isn't the case for you, don't be shocked if some of your friends and family pull away. They often do this in an effort to protect their own emotions.

- After the death of someone loved, we often ask ourselves, "Why go on living?" "Will my life have meaning now?" "Where is God in this?" Spiritual questions such as these are natural and necessary but also draining. If you are feeling spiritual discomfort, you may want to talk with a clergyperson or spiritual counselor.

- Basically, your grief may affect every aspect of your life. Nothing may feel "normal" right now. If this is true for you, don't be alarmed. Just trust that in time, you will find peace and comfort again.

CARPE DIEM:

If you've felt physically affected by your grief, see a doctor this week.
Sometimes it's comforting to receive a clean bill of health.

8.
EMBRACE YOUR SPIRITUALITY

- Above all, grief is a journey of the soul. It demands you to consider why people live, why people die, and what gives life meaning. These are the most spiritual questions we have language to form.

- For many people, formal places of worship—churches, synagogues, mosques—offer a safe place and a ritualized process for discovering and embracing their spirituality. If you don't belong to a place of worship, perhaps now is a good time to join.

- Try to schedule some spiritual time into each day.

- For me, spending time alone in nature provides both the solitude and the beautiful evidence of God's existence that I need to nurture my soul. This "exile time" helps restore my soul and gives me the energy to cope with the demands of my day.

- Since your spouse died, you may have found yourself contemplating your own eventual death. This is very common. After all, you were partners in life. It's only natural to wonder if you'll be partners after life.

- We grow, we learn; the spiritual path is a lifetime unfolding process. The death of your spouse may inspire this spiritual unfolding. Make the effort to embrace your spirituality and it will embrace you back by inspiring you with a sense of peace, hope, and healing.

CARPE DIEM:
Perhaps you have a friend who seems spiritually grounded. Talk to this person about his beliefs and spiritual experiences. Ask him how he learned to nurture his spirituality.

9.
LET GO OF DESTRUCTIVE MYTHS ABOUT GRIEF AND MOURNING

- Unknowingly, you have probably internalized many of our society's harmful myths about grief and mourning.

- Here are some to let go of:
  - I need to be strong and carry on.
  - Tears are a sign of weakness.
  - I need to get over my grief.
  - Death is something we don't talk about.

- Sometimes these myths will cause you to feel guilty about or ashamed of your true thoughts and feelings.

- Your grief is your grief. It's normal and necessary. Allow it to be what it is. Allow it to last as long as it lasts. Strive to be an authentic mourner—one who openly and honestly expresses what you think and feel.

CARPE DIEM:
Help de-mythologize grief by talking to your friends and family about grief and mourning. Let them know that their feelings about your spouse's death are normal and necessary. Share how you've been feeling.

10.
TELL THE STORY, OVER AND OVER AGAIN IF NECESSARY

- Acknowledging a death is a painful, ongoing need that we meet in doses, over time. A vital part of healing in grief is often "telling the story" over and over again.

- The "story" relates the circumstances surrounding the death, reviewing the relationship, describing aspects of the personality of the spouse who died, and sharing memories, good and bad.

- It's as if each time we tell the story, it becomes a little more real. It also becomes a more integrated part of who we are.

- Find people who are willing to listen to you tell your story, over and over again if necessary, without judgment.

CARPE DIEM:
Tell the story to someone today in the form of a letter. Perhaps you can write and send this letter to a friend who lives far away. If you are not a letter writer, find a trusted friend to "talk out" the story. You will know who will be willing to listen and who won't.

11.

START EACH NEW DAY WITH A MEDITATION OR PRAYER

- For many widows, waking up in the morning is the hardest part of their day. It's as if each time you awaken, you must confront anew the realization that your lifemate has died.

- Starting the day off with tears and a heavy heart, day in and day out, is so draining. Yet it may be a necessary part of your grief journey, especially in the early weeks and months after the death.

- Later, however, you may begin to have the power to set the tone for your day by praying or meditating.

- When you wake up, stretch before getting out of bed. Feel the blood coursing through your body. Listen to the hum of your consciousness.

- Repeat a simple phrase or prayer to yourself, such as: "Today I will live and love fully. Today I will appreciate my life." You might also offer words of gratitude: "Thank you, God, for giving me this day. Help me to appreciate it and to make it count."

CARPE DIEM:

Write a simple affirmation or prayer on a piece of paper and tape it to your bedroom mirror. Tomorrow morning when you get up, concentrate on this phrase for one minute.

12.
WALK SIDE-BY-SIDE WITH YOUR GRIEF

- Our society teaches us that emotional pain is to be avoided, not embraced, yet it is only in moving toward our grief that we can be healed.

- As Helen Keller once said, "The only way to get to the other side is to go through the door."

- To the extent possible, walk side-by-side with your grief. Don't let it always be the fickle leader, yanking you down one miserable path after another. Resolve to take an active role in your healing. Don't think of yourself as a powerless victim or as helpless in the face of grief. Instead, empower yourself to "do something" with your grief—to mourn it, to express it outside yourself, to find ways to help yourself heal.

- But don't expect to lead your grief all the time, either. You can't always "direct" your thoughts and feelings. Instead, lean into them and listen to them. Then take your grief by the hand and walk shoulder-to-shoulder.

- Be suspicious if you find yourself thinking that you're "doing well" since the death. Sometimes "doing well" means you're avoiding your pain.

CARPE DIEM:
Today, do something to confront and express your grief. Maybe it's time to tell someone close to you how you've really been feeling.

13.
ACKNOWLEDGE ALL THE LOSSES THIS DEATH HAS WROUGHT

- When a spouse dies, you lose not only the physical presence of your husband or wife, but also a part of your self—the part that you gave to the person you loved so very much.

- With the death of a spouse comes many other losses. Depending on the unique nature of your relationship with your partner, you may have lost your best friend, your lover, your soulmate. You may also have lost your dance partner, your traveling companion, your chef, your gardener, your chauffeur, your comedian, or your accountant.

- What varied roles did your spouse play in your life?

- Allowing yourself to acknowledge the many levels of loss the death has brought to your life will help you move forward in your grief journey.

CARPE DIEM:
Name the things that you've lost or events you'll mourn
in the future as a result of your spouse's death.

14.
ALLOW FOR FEELINGS OF
UNFINISHED BUSINESS

- The death of a spouse often brings about feelings of unfinished business. Things we never did, things we didn't get to say, things we wish we hadn't.

- Allow yourself to think and feel through these "if onlys" and "should haves." You may never be able to fully resolve these issues, but if you permit yourself to mourn them, you will become reconciled to them.

- Is there something you wanted to say to your partner but never did? Write him or her a letter that openly expresses your thoughts and feelings—but only when you're ready. Or, it may be more natural for you to "talk out" these things with a trusted friend or counselor.

- If you know other widows, talk with them about your regrets and "if onlys." They probably have similar feelings. In fact, you may be surprised at how closely the experiences of others mirror those of your own. Knowing that others have gone through the same thing may help you feel more secure and at peace.

CARPE DIEM:
Take this opportunity to tie up any loose ends you may
have with someone who's still alive. Express your
feelings and renew your relationship.

15.
FORGIVE YOURSELF

- You probably made some mistakes in your relationship with your spouse. We all have. None of us is the perfect husband or wife.

- The "if-onlys" can consume you if you're not vigilant. If only he hadn't run that errand (before the car accident)... If only she had seen the doctor sooner... If only I hadn't said that... The "if-onlys" are normal and need to be explored. However, after allowing yourself to feel them, you must eventually let them go.

- Were you ever mean or spiteful to your partner? Did you lie to him or make poor decisions that adversely affected you both? Did you fail to support him when he needed you? Were you ever unfaithful?

- And your spouse? Did she ever treat you badly or fail you in any way?

- Forgive your spouse her shortcomings and while you're at it, forgive yourself. As you now know, life is too short to bear grudges, even against yourself. Imperfect love, which is the best we humans can manage, is infinitely better than no love at all.

- Widows are often engulfed by another unique type of regret: survivor guilt. Why did your spouse die and not you? Why were you the one to go on living? Survivor guilt, like all types of guilt in grief, is normal and may be necessary for you to explore. Perhaps in the long run you will come to embrace the peace of the Serenity Prayer:
  God grant me the serenity to accept the things I cannot change,
  the courage to change the things I can,
  and the wisdom to know the difference.

CARPE DIEM:
Is there something you've been feeling guilty about? Forgive yourself. Write your transgression on a slip of paper, tear it up into tiny pieces, and toss it into the wind.

16.
COMBAT THE LONELINESS

- The person you sat down to dinner with every night with is now gone. The person you spent your free time with. The person you shared your bed with. The person who knew you best.

- If you are childless or your children have left home, you may find yourself feeling lonely much of the time. There's no one to talk to, no one to share a meal with, no one to hold.

- Grieving spouses tell me that the way they combat loneliness is by making it a point to interact with others. Get out of your house, if only to go for a walk and say hello to your neighbors. Attend your place of worship. Rediscover former hobbies. Volunteer. Join a club or organization—especially one that involves not just couples but singles, too. And be sure to make plans to be with people you care about.

- My mother, age 76, has a weekly appointment at her local YMCA to go swimming with other seniors. Mom has also taken up watercolor painting again—a long-ago hobby that went by the wayside when she was raising children and being a wife.

- If you have children at home, you may still feel lonely. You love your children, of course, but being with your children isn't the same as being with a peer and lover. Don't make the mistake of inappropriately burdening young children with your adult thoughts and feelings. Instead, find ways to interact with other adults.

- Finally, don't confuse being alone with loneliness. Part of your grief journey will involve learning how to be alone again—and appreciate it. Devote some time to thinking about what YOU like to do, then use your alone time to do it.

CARPE DIEM:

Even if you don't feel like it, call someone today and invite them to dinner. You could prepare a meal at home or you could treat at a nearby restaurant. During the meal and afterwards, pay attention to how you're feeling. If having company helps you feel less lonely, commit to yourself to arrange lunch or dinner with others at least once a week.

17.
REACH OUT TO OTHERS FOR HELP

- Perhaps the most compassionate thing you can do for yourself at this difficult time is to reach out for help from others. Mourning, by definition, means "shared social response to loss." Don't try to do this alone; it can't be done!

- Think of it this way: Grieving may be the hardest work you have ever done. And hard work is less burdensome when others lend a hand. Life's greatest challenges—getting through school, raising children, pursuing a career—are in many ways team efforts. So it should be with mourning.

- Sharing your pain with others won't make it disappear, but it will, over time, make it more bearable. You may find it particularly helpful to talk to other widows. From our common bond comes hope for our mutual healing.

- Reaching out for help also connects you to other people and strengthens the bonds of love that make life seem worth living again.

CARPE DIEM:
Call a close friend who may have distanced himself from you since the death and tell him how much you need him right now. Suggest specific ways he can help.

18.

IDENTIFY THREE PEOPLE YOU CAN TURN TO ANYTIME YOU NEED A FRIEND

• You may have many people who care about you but few who are able to be good companions in grief.

• Identify three people whom you think can be there for you in the coming weeks and months.

• Don't assume that others will help. Even normally compassionate people sometimes find it hard to be present to others in grief.

• I find that after a death, you can usually divide the people you know into three groups. The neutral group won't harm you in your grief, nor will they generally be of much help. The harmful group will make you feel worse by what they say or do. (Yes, sometimes these can even be family members or former best friends.) And the helpful group will be available to you and supportive of your need to mourn. Try to spend time with those who help and set boundaries with those who are harmful to you right now.

CARPE DIEM:

Call these three people and ask them outright: Could you please help me? Tell them you mainly need to spend time with them and talk to them freely.

19.
UNDERSTAND THE SIX NEEDS OF MOURNING

Need #1: Acknowledge the reality of the death.

• This first need of mourning requires you to gently confront the difficult reality that your spouse is dead and will never physically be present to you again.

• Whether the death was sudden or anticipated, acknowledging the full reality of the loss may occur over weeks and months.

• You will first acknowledge the reality of the loss with your head. Only over time will you come to acknowledge it with your heart.

• At times you may push away the reality of your spouse's death. This is normal. You will come to integrate the reality, in doses, as you are ready.

CARPE DIEM:
Tell someone about the death today. You might talk about the circumstances of the death or review the relationship you had with your husband or wife. Talking about it will help you work on this important need.

20.
UNDERSTAND THE SIX NEEDS OF MOURNING

Need #2: Embrace the pain of the loss.

- This need requires mourners to embrace the pain of their loss—something we naturally don't want to do. It is easier to avoid, repress, or push away the pain of grief than it is to confront it.

- It is in embracing your grief, however, that you will learn to reconcile yourself to it.

- Always remember that your pain is normal and necessary. You are not being "overly emotional" if you feel devastated after the death of someone loved.

- You will probably need to "dose" yourself in embracing your pain. If you were to allow in all the pain at once, you could not survive.

CARPE DIEM:
If you feel up to it, allow yourself a time for embracing pain today. Dedicate 15 minutes to thinking about and feeling the loss. Reach out to someone who doesn't try to take your pain away and spend some time with him.

21.
UNDERSTAND THE SIX NEEDS OF MOURNING

Need #3: Remember the spouse who died.

• When someone loved dies, they live on in us through memory.

• To heal, you need to actively remember your spouse and commemorate the life that was lived.

• Never let anyone take your memories away in a misguided attempt to save you from pain. It's good for you to continue to display photos of your husband or wife. It's good for you to talk about your partner's life and death. It's good for you to hold onto objects that belonged to your spouse.

• Remembering the past makes hoping for the future possible. As E.M. Forster wrote, "Unless we remember we cannot understand." And, as Kierkegaard noted, "Life is lived forward but understood backward."

CARPE DIEM:
Brainstorm a list of characteristics or memories of your spouse.
Write as fast as you can for 10 minutes (or more), then
put away your list for later reflection.

22.
UNDERSTAND THE SIX NEEDS
OF MOURNING

Need #4: Develop a new self-identity

• A large part of your self-identity was formed by the relationship you had with your partner who died. Perhaps for much of your adult life, you were part of a couple, one of two. You were half of something whole.

• Now you are single. Your other "half" is gone. You are one of one. The way you defined yourself and the way society defined you have changed.

• This change will take some getting used to. You may struggle with this process of redefinition for months or years. Who are you now? Who are you without a partner? You need to re-anchor yourself, to reconstruct your self-identity. This is arduous and painful work.

• Something to keep in mind as you consider your new identity is that you can and will exist alone. Being single is a different reality; it is not a "lesser" reality. Of course, you probably would not have chosen to be single. You may wish things could be as they were. But one is also a whole number. You are, all by yourself, a child of God.

• Many mourners discover that as they work on developing a new self-identity, they ultimately reveal a better, truer self. For example, some widows find they are more caring or less judgmental. Many find ways to help others.

CARPE DIEM:
Write out a response to this prompt: I used to be
_____. Now that _____ died, I am
_____. This makes me feel _____.
Keep writing as long as you want.

23.
UNDERSTAND THE SIX NEEDS OF MOURNING

Need #5: Search for meaning.

• When someone we love dies, we naturally question the meaning and purpose of life and death.

• "Why?" questions may surface uncontrollably and often precede "How" questions. Questions such as "Why did my husband die this way?" or "Why did my wife have to get sick?" often come before "How will I go on living?"

• You will probably question your philosophy of life and explore religious and spiritual values as you work on this need.

• Remember that having faith or spirituality does not negate your need to mourn. Even if you believe in life after death or that your spouse has gone to "a better place," you still have the right and the need to mourn this significant loss in your life. "Blessed are those who mourn for they shall be comforted."

CARPE DIEM:
Write down a list of "why" questions that may have surfaced for you since the death. Find a friend or counselor who will explore these questions with you without thinking she has to give you answers.

24.
UNDERSTAND THE SIX NEEDS OF MOURNING

Need #6: Receive ongoing support from others.

- As mourners, we need the love and understanding of others if we are to heal.

- If you feel dependent on others right now, don't feel ashamed. Instead, revel in the knowledge that others care about you. Acknowledging your need for support is not a weakness, it is a strength.

- Unfortunately, our society places too much value on "carrying on" and "doing well" after a death. So, many grieving spouses are abandoned by their friends and family soon after the death.

- Grief is a process, not an event, and you will need the continued support of your friends and family for weeks, months, and years.

CARPE DIEM:

Sometimes your friends want to support you but don't know how. Tell them. The next time someone says to you, "Let me know how I can help," offer a suggestion or two. Tell them you need help with your lawn or keeping up with laundry—whatever is overwhelming you right now. When given specific tasks, most people are more than happy to help.

25.
KNOW THAT GRIEF DOES NOT PROCEED IN ORDERLY, PREDICTABLE "STAGES"

- Though the "Needs of Mourning" (Ideas 19-24) are numbered 1-6, grief is not an orderly progression towards healing. Don't fall into the trap of thinking your grief journey will be predictable or always forward-moving.

- Usually, grief hurts more before it hurts less.

- You will probably experience a multitude of different emotions in a wave-like fashion. You will also likely encounter more than one need of mourning at the same time.

- Be compassionate with yourself as you experience your own unique grief journey.

CARPE DIEM:
Has anyone told you that you are in this or that "stage" of grief? Ignore this usually well-intended advice. Don't allow yourself or anyone else to compartmentalize your grief.

26.
TURN OVER THE FINANCIAL REINS FOR NOW

- The death of a spouse often has many financial repercussions. Perhaps the family wage-earner has died. Or maybe an illness resulted in staggering medical bills. Often funeral and burial expenses also impact the family budget.

- Emotionally and cognitively, you may not be able to focus on finances right now. Your grief and your family—definitely your top priorities at the moment—may require all your energy.

- But now is not the time to let your finances slide, either. Missed mortgage payments, mounting medical bills, and other financial foibles can create nightmarish, long-term problems.

- Ask someone you trust to help you monitor your finances and pay bills. You probably know someone who is good with money and who would be happy to step in as temporary accountant.

- My father was an accountant and actually enjoyed handling the family finances—for which my mother, who didn't like balancing the checkbook, was grateful. Assuming that she should now handle her own finances when she never did before would have been a mistake. My sister now helps Mom with day-to-day bills and I coordinate her longer-term investments.

- Now is not the time to make any major financial decisions, however, unless absolutely necessary. If at all possible, try to wait at least a year to make any significant changes in your life. Of course, if you must make major changes for health or financial reasons, make them and know that you did your best.

CARPE DIEM:
Gather up your checkbook, bank statements, unpaid bills, and any other financial papers you may need into one stack today. Ask someone for help. If you're not comfortable asking a friend or family member, find a personal accountant in the Yellow Pages and phone today for an appointment.

27.
RECOGNIZE THAT YOUR FRIENDSHIPS WILL PROBABLY CHANGE

- Widows often tell me how surprised and hurt they feel when friends fall away after the death of a spouse. "I found out who my friends really are," they say.

- Married friends, especially, may have a hard time relating to you now. Those who are used to relating to you "couple-to-couple" may not know how or if to include you any longer.

- Know that just as you are, your friends are doing the best they can. They surely still care about you, but they are also grieving the death of your spouse. And more to the point, your presence pricks at their fears of their own widowhood.

- Your non-married friends may also have a hard time connecting with you now. As a culture, we're not good about grief. We don't know what to say and we don't know how to act. So, unfortunately, we avoid.

- The best way for you to respond in the face of faltering friendships is to be proactive and honest. Even though you're the one who's grieving, you may need to be the one to phone your friends and keep in touch.

- By contrast, maybe you are one of the fortunate people who feel tremendous support and love from your friends after the death of a spouse. If so, rejoice that you have such wise and wonderful friends.

CARPE DIEM:
If a friend you particularly care about has been distancing himself from you since the death, call him and invite him out to lunch or for a drink. Sometimes people truly care but can't bring themselves to make that first connection. They're often relieved when you do it for them and after that, they're better able to stay in touch.

28.
LET OTHERS TAKE CARE OF YOU

- Some of your friends and family may respond to the death by trying to take care of you. They may bring you meals, run your errands, offer to clean your house. Let them! Consider yourself fortunate to be so well loved.

- You may find yourself feeling passive and childlike. You may need help with simple day-to-day chores and decisions. This is a normal, temporary grief response. On the other hand, you may feel angry that everyone is trying to babysit you. Try to understand that they're only trying to help. Discuss your feelings without lashing out.

- If your parents are still alive, you may find them trying to coddle you and care for you—to parent you. Understand that this is a normal response on their part. Regardless of how "old" you are, you are still their child and they may want to nurture and support you. Tell them, gently, what you find helpful and what you do not.

- If your children are teens or adults, they may also try to take care of you. While it can be a blessing to have adult children around to help you through this difficult time, watch out for inappropriately burdening teenagers and very young adults. It is most unfair to your children to be expected to fill in for the parent who died. Yes, everyone in the family may need to pitch in more now, but young people should NOT be asked to take on roles and responsibilities beyond their years.

CARPE DIEM:
Write a brief thank you note to someone who has helped you recently. Tell her how much you appreciate her presence in your life.

29.
IF YOUR HUSBAND HAS DIED, CONSIDER THIS:

- Wives, especially, often tell me how lonely they feel after their husband dies. Women often crave the day-to-day companionship a partner provides. They miss having someone to talk to and even someone to take care of. Women also tend to place more of an emphasis on their role as wife and mother. Their self-identities are often largely shaped by their relationships with their family.

- Depending on how responsibilities were divided in your home, you may need help with certain tasks. What did your husband take care of? Did he handle the finances? Mow the lawn? Service the cars?

- Your husband may have also played a certain social or emotional role in your household. Was he the "outgoing one" or the "listener"? In life you probably complemented each other. In death you will mourn the loss of your other half. In my mother and father's relationship, Dad was always the more social of the two. He was the planner and the relationship-maker. When he died, this social area was more challenging for my mom.

- Who was the breadwinner in your family? If your husband earned most or all of your family's income, you may have to re-enter the workforce. Or, as is more typical today, if your husband earned part of the family income, you may be struggling financially on your salary alone. See an uncommissioned credit counselor or a financial planner to help establish a sound fiscal plan.

- Widows tend to remain single much longer than widowers. Many never recommit to a serious relationship. If this is your choice, that's fine—as long as you are choosing what makes you happiest.

CARPE DIEM:
Think about what being a "wife" meant to you. Write a list of what was most important to you in your role as wife. Write a second list of what is most important to you now. Consider how you will refocus your energies on this second list.

30.
IF YOUR WIFE HAS DIED,
CONSIDER THIS:

- "I feel so lost without her" is a common comment I hear from husbands. It seems that outside of the husband's work sphere, wives tend to be in the driver's seat. Your wife may have managed your household and your social affairs. You may feel at a loss about how to spend your time and get the things done that need to be done.

- Because, on average, men die younger than women, our society has far fewer widowers than widows. In the U.S., the ratio is about one-to-five and gets even more disproportionate as age increases. You may find that you don't know many other widowers and that being a man alone is a particularly difficult role to play socially.

- Consider joining groups in which single people participate. If you join a sports team, for example, or a civic organization (such as the Kiwanis), you may form friendships with other men (or women) who share your interests and are more available than their married counterparts for social activities during the evening or on weekends.

- If you have children at home, you may need help with their care. Please, get help. Ask your friends to take on more of the carpooling. If you can afford it, hire a housekeeper. And most important, avoid inappropriately burdening your children with adult responsibilities.

- Widowers tend to get involved in serious relationships or remarry much sooner then widows. Take care not to act too quickly. Go slow! I often say that there are no rewards for speed.

CARPE DIEM:
Find at least one other widower you can talk to about your circumstances. Ask him how he managed during those early months and years after the death.

31.

IF YOUR SPOUSE DIED AFTER AN EXTENDED ILLNESS OR DECLINE, KNOW THAT FEELINGS OF RELIEF ARE PERFECTLY NORMAL

- Due to today's medical advances, people are living much longer than they did in past centuries. Sometimes, modern medicines and machines keep people alive to enjoy life for many extra years. But those same medicines and machines can prolong suffering.

- If your husband or wife died after an extended illness or decline, what you may feel above all else is a tremendous sense of relief. If you cared for or spent time with your spouse while he or she suffered, you may even have wished—prayed!—for a swift death.

- My own father died after a two-year illness, during which my mother watched him dwindle from the man she once knew. This was very painful for her. Toward the end she even said out loud, "If he is going to die, why doesn't he go ahead and do it." Of course, this wasn't said out of a lack of love. This was more about her feelings of helplessness to stop what was happening.

- Feelings of relief after a prolonged or painful illness is ended by death are common. It is perfectly normal and understandable to want your partner's suffering to end and your life to return to normal. Of course, you've probably found that your life is not "normal" anymore. Your spouse has died. Your life is forever changed. And even though you were anticipating the death, you may still feel shocked when it actually happens.

- If the death was recent, you may worry if all you seem to remember or think about is your partner's suffering and death. Rest assured that in time, you will once again recall happier, gentler memories.

CARPE DIEM:

Call or write a note to someone else who was involved in your spouse's care during the last days or weeks. Share your feelings with this person and thank her for her concern and help.

32.
IF YOU HELPED CARE FOR YOUR ILL SPOUSE, GIVE YOURSELF TIME TO RECUPERATE

- If your spouse was terminally ill, you may have had to shoulder multiple burdens. One was your anticipatory grief; you knew that he or she was going to die and, over time, you were forced to come to terms with that. Another was likely your spouse's physical care. While certainly your spouse was cared for by doctors and nurses, you may well have been the primary day-to-day, hour-to-hour caregiver—in addition to your usual roles as parent, chief cook and bottle washer, career-person, etc.

- Caring for someone who is sick is physically as well as emotionally draining. You may be exhausted. During my dad's illness, my mother occasionally said that she might die before he did. This was an expression of how physically and emotionally exhausted she was.

- When a husband or wife you have been caring for dies, you may feel gratified that you "did everything you could" or you may feel a sense of failure. You may not know what do with yourself now that your days are no longer consumed by caring for your spouse. You may feel a sense of loss now that you are no longer needed.

- Your life changed when your spouse became ill and it has changed again now that he or she has died. Give yourself some time and space to absorb this change. Go into neutral and lower your self-expectations. Concentrate on caring for yourself right now.

CARPE DIEM:
This weekend or one weekend soon, schedule nothing. Plan to putter around the house, sleep, watch movies, read books. Rest your body and your mind and your soul.

33.

IF YOUR SPOUSE DIED SUDDENLY, LOOK FOR WAYS TO EMBRACE THE REALITY OF THE DEATH

- The sudden death of a spouse, like any sudden death, comes as a shock. For a while, the death may seem completely unreal and dreamlike.

- Sudden, unexpected death often makes the search for meaning need (see Idea 23) more difficult. If this is the case for you, be patient with yourself.

- This heightened sense of disbelief protects you in the early days and weeks after the death. If your mind were to force you to confront the reality all at once, you could not survive. I often say, "Thank God for shock!"

- But later, as you are ready, confronting the reality of the death in doses will help you heal. Encourage yourself to talk about the death. Look at photos of your partner. Visit the place of the death. Talk with the last people to speak with your spouse.

- If your spouse completed suicide, your grief journey will be particularly difficult. Coming to terms with the suicide of someone loved can take much longer, and much more grief work, than other types of death. I encourage suicide survivors to seek extra support from an experienced grief counselor and/or a suicide support group.

- Embracing the reality of the death can be painful, but even more painful in the long run is pushing it away. To come to terms with this sudden death is to come to terms with continued life.

CARPE DIEM:

If your spouse died suddenly, close your eyes and imagine his or her last hours. What was she doing when she died? What was the weather like? What were you doing? What thoughts and feelings were you able to convey? What thoughts or words would you have conveyed to him at that moment if you could have? Send those thoughts his way right now.

34.
CONJURE UP YOUR SPOUSE

- Sometimes when you're missing your precious husband or wife, it helps to call his or her presence to your mind and to your heart.

- Close your eyes and remember your spouse's face. See her smiling at you. Look at the lines around her eyes and the sweep of her hair. Recall her eyes, her nose, her lips. If you have a difficult time with this visualization, get out several of your favorite pictures of your spouse.

- Picture your spouse's body. Remember his arms and his torso and his legs. In your mind's eye, see his freckles and his scars.

- Also recall the smell and feel of your spouse's skin. Feel the touch of her lips on yours.

- With practice, you'll get better at conjuring up your spouse's physical presence. This exercise is not weird or morbid; it's simply a way to help you keep his memory alive.

- If this is too overwhelming or painful to you right now, come back to this activity at a later date. Remember you are on a journey and you will be ready for different experiences at different times.

CARPE DIEM:
Right now, close your eyes and imagine yourself looking into your spouse's eyes. He is smiling at you. Smile back.

35.
ASK YOUR SPOUSE FOR ADVICE

- Many husbands and wives consult each other about decisions big and little. You may have asked your husband's opinion about your clothing and your career. He may have asked yours about finances and childrearing.

- One of the most beautiful things about marriage is this emotional intimacy. Who else knew you so well?

- Now that your spouse is gone, you may feel at a loss about where to turn when you need to talk out a challenge or concern in your life. I hope you have friends you can be open and honest with. But even so, you naturally miss your spouse's listening ear and open heart.

- If you believe that your spouse still exists somewhere, somehow, go ahead and ask her for advice. Talk to her picture or simply talk silently to her in your head.

- Imagine what he would say. Often you know what his answer would be and it's comforting to "hear" his response in your mind. Or watch for an answer —a "sign" from your spouse—to emerge in your life.

CARPE DIEM:

If you're facing a big decision, ask your spouse for advice. Allow yourself to consider what she would say while realizing that you must ultimately make the decision that works best for you here and now.

36.
KEEP IT REAL WITH YOUR CHILDREN

- Can you be a grieving spouse and a parent to grieving children at the same time? Yes you can, but you'll need help. Sometimes your own grief will have to take precedence. If your grief has left you with little energy to devote to your kids, ask other family members or friends to help out. Whatever you do, don't allow your children to be neglected at this critical time. Remember—it takes a village to raise a child.

- If your children are young, the most important thing is for you to be open with them. They may ask you how their mom or dad died. They might express fears about their own death or yours. Give them gentle but honest answers in language they'll understand.

- If your children are grown up and on their own, you may need to make an extra effort to reach out to them after the death. You might think they need little support and they might think you're doing "fine"—but chances are that both of you are wrong. Initiate an open and ongoing dialogue.

- You will probably discover that your children will mourn in different ways. One child may be openly expressive, while another may try to conceal his feelings from you. My rule of thirds (see Idea 18) can often apply even to your own children! You will probably find that you can mourn more openly with some of your kids.

- Within reason, it's good to model your own grief in your children's presence. Talk about memories, cry, tell stories, look at photos—all these behaviors let your children know that expressing their grief outside of themselves is healthy and healing.

- If your family hasn't been doing such a good job of openly mourning this death, it's not too late to start. Schedule a family meeting and ask everyone to share their feelings about the death.

CARPE DIEM:
Make an effort to talk to your children today about their grief as well as your own.

37.

IF YOU ARE ANGRY, FIND APPROPRIATE WAYS TO EXPRESS YOUR ANGER

- For some grieving spouses, feelings of shock and disbelief after the death are followed by anger.

- You may be angry at medical caregivers, your family, your friends, even your spouse.

- Feelings of anger at the spouse who died are quite common. Perhaps you're angry that he didn't quit smoking or didn't see the doctor sooner. Maybe you're mad that she left you behind. Or maybe you're feeling it's unfair that you have to take on so many extra responsibilities.

- Anger is normal and necessary. It's our way of protesting a reality we don't like. It helps us survive. And anger is far sounder than a resignation to despair. Anger and feelings of protest challenge relationships, where despair severs or cuts off relationships. Anger may be frightening, but indifference is deadening.

- Watch out for people who prescribe anger to you. Some people have anger, some don't. What about you? If the shoe fits, wear it. If it doesn't, don't feel the need to put it on.

- Since my dad died, my mother has expressed some anger about all the things he did for her (paying bills, making major decisions), which at the time, when he was alive, she seemed to enjoy. Her present anger is more about her protest that he is no longer here to do these things for her than it is about true anger that he did them. Underlying our anger is often our feelings of hurt, pain, fear, and frustration. Do you have a similar example in your own grief?

CARPE DIEM:

Today, do something physical to vent your anger. Go for a
fast walk or punch a boxing bag. Smash a tennis ball
against a practice wall over and over.

38.

IF YOU ARE UPSET ABOUT THE MEDICAL CARE YOUR SPOUSE RECEIVED, EXPRESS THOSE FEELINGS

- The modern medical system can be exasperating for patients and their families. If your spouse was ill before she died, she may have endured countless doctor visits, tests, diagnoses, and treatments. My own father saw eight different doctors during his two-year illness. We often felt like he was being bounced around from specialist to specialist. In part, what was really happening was that both the doctors and my family were looking for ways to change the reality that my father was dying.

- As with my father, modern medicine was not able to "cure" your husband or wife. You may feel frustrated that the treatments didn't work. You may feel angry at busy doctors, who perhaps seemed brusque or unthorough. You may feel bad decisions were made. You may feel your spouse suffered too much or too long.

- If you harbor bad feelings about your partner's medical care, find a way to express those feelings. I'm not talking about frivolous lawsuits here. I'm simply suggesting that talking out your grievances about your spouse's medical care may help you move beyond them to the real work of mourning the death itself.

- Write a letter to the doctor or practice or hospital expressing your concerns, even if you never send it. Do you personally know someone in the medical field? Talk to this person about your feelings; he may be able to provide some "inside" perspective. Or talk out your feelings with your family.

CARPE DIEM:
While you may feel upset about some aspect of your spouse's care, you probably feel grateful about another. Write a note of thanks to a caregiver who was particularly compassionate or helpful.

39.
TURN TO YOUR FAMILY

- In today's mobile, disconnected society, many people have lost touch with the gift of family. Your friends may come and go, but family, as they say, is forever.

- If you're emotionally close to members of your family, you're probably already reaching out to them for support. Allow them to be there for you. Let them in. Accept their love and support and help.

- If you're not emotionally close to your family, perhaps now is the time to open closed doors. Call a family member you haven't spoken to for a while. Hop in a car or on a plane and make a long overdue visit.

- Since my father's death, my mother has reconnected with a special cousin from childhood. They have even gone on a trip together. Is there someone you could try to "reconnect" with?

- Don't feel bad if you have to be the initiator; instead, expend your energy by writing that first letter or making that first phone call.

CARPE DIEM:
Call a family member you feel close to today. Make plans to visit this person soon.

40.
DO WHAT FEELS RIGHT WITH YOUR SPOUSE'S BELONGINGS

- Knowing what to do with your spouse's belongings—and when to do it—can be difficult.

- As with all things in grief, there is no one right way to handle this issue. You must do what feels right for you and your family.

- Ask a friend or family member to help you. This is often too large—and too emotional—a task to handle alone.

- When you're ready to sort through your partner's belongings (and do go slowly; there are no rewards for speed!), consider which items might be meaningful later on to you or to others. Don't dispose of things in haste; you won't be able to get them back later.

- Be sure to check in with your children or other relatives about any desire they may have for belongings. I have my dad's baseball glove, which came with many treasured memories of playing catch with him in the backyard throughout my childhood. I also have his Purdue University hat. These are not just simple "belongings." These are precious links to my dad.

- Do keep at least a box of special items just for yourself.

- Some widows I have had the honor of counseling have done creative things like taking different pieces of clothing, cutting them up and having them made into a special quilt or blanket. Can you think of anything creative you could do?

CARPE DIEM:
Bring some of the smaller special items that belonged to your spouse into a frame shop and ask for help in creating a special shadow box. My Uncle Bob did this with my Aunt Helen's paint supplies (brush, a palette, etc.) after she died.

41.

RELEASE ANY BAD FEELINGS OR REGRETS YOU MAY HAVE ABOUT THE FUNERAL AND BURIAL

- The funeral is a wonderful means of expressing our beliefs, thoughts, and feelings about the death of someone loved.

- Funerals help us acknowledge the reality of the death, give testimony to the life of the person who died, express our grief, support each other, and embrace our faith and beliefs about life and death.

- Yet for many mourners, funeral planning is difficult. Funeral and burial decisions may have been made quickly, while you were still in deep shock and disbelief. Sometimes some of these decisions seem wrong with the benefit of hindsight.

- If you harbor any negative feelings about your spouse's funeral or memorial service, know this: You and everyone else who was a part of the service did the best they could do at the time. You cannot change what happened, but you can talk about what happened and share your thoughts and feelings with someone who cares.

- Remember, if you didn't have a funeral, it's never too late. (It's also never too late to hold an additional memorial service.) Look for someone who is a "ritual specialist" and can help you create a meaningful ceremony to remember your spouse. Perhaps a tree-planting ceremony or a small gathering on the anniversary of the death could be a forum for sharing memories and prayer. I often say, "When words are inadequate, have a ceremony."

- On the other hand, you may feel that your husband or wife's funeral was a wonderful, healing experience worthy of the life he or she lived and the love you shared. If so, be sure to thank the people who made it possible.

CARPE DIEM:

If you harbor regrets or anger about your spouse's funeral and burial, talk about these feelings with someone today. Perhaps the two of you together can create an "action plan" to help make things better.

47

42.
PREPARE FOR YOUR OWN EVENTUAL DEATH

- As a society, we're not very good at death. We don't like to think about it, we don't like to talk about it, and we certainly don't like to plan for it. But now that death has knocked at your door, maybe you're ready to face it more openly and honestly.

- Even if you are likely years or decades away from death yourself, talk to your family—especially your children, if you have any— about your hopes and fears. Talk to them as if you only have days to live. Tell them how you feel about them. Tell them your hopes for them. Tell them your regrets. If apologies are in order, tell them you're sorry.

- See an attorney to make sure your estate is in order. Do you have life insurance? Do you have an up-to-date will? Does someone have information on all your accounts and belongings?

- Consider pre-planning your funeral. While funerals are for the living and shouldn't be rigidly pre-planned, it might help your family to know whether you'd prefer to be buried or cremated and where your remains should be buried or scattered. You might also write down a few suggestions about music you find meaningful or old friends to notify.

- You may also want to take care of financial arrangements for yourself. Set aside some money in a specially designated account or pre-pay through a funeral home.

CARPE DIEM:

Write a note to each of your children telling them how special they are to you and relating good memories. Seal the notes in individual envelopes marked with each child's name. Place the notes with your will or other important papers. Someday—perhaps years or decades from now—your children will find and cherish these loving messages.

43.
CRY

- Tears are a natural cleansing and healing mechanism. It's OK to cry. In fact, it's good to cry when you feel like it. What's more, tears are a form of mourning. They are sacred!

- On the other hand, don't feel bad if you aren't crying a lot. Not everyone is a crier.

- You may find that those around you are uncomfortable with your tears. As a society, we're often not so good at witnessing others in pain.

- Explain to your friends and family that you need to cry right now and that they can help by allowing you to.

- You may find yourself crying at unexpected times or places. If you need to, or feel safer doing so, excuse yourself and retreat to somewhere private. But don't feel shame; you are entitled to your tears.

- You may find yourself crying about things you see or hear that you haven't cared about in the past. These tears are called "borrowed tears." Go ahead and experience them and be glad you can.

- Sometimes it helps to allow yourself a private time and place to cry every day, maybe when you come home from work or when you first get up in the morning. Knowing that you'll have this "crying time" may free you to function better the rest of the day.

CARPE DIEM:

If you feel like it, have a good cry today. Find a safe place to embrace your pain and cry as long and as hard as you want to.

44.
REACH OUT AND TOUCH

- For many people, physical contact with another human being is healing. It has been recognized since ancient times as having transformative, healing powers.

- Have you hugged anyone lately? Held someone's hand? Put your arm around another human being?

- For married people who have lost a spouse, being without someone to hug and hold is often a big part of their grief. You may have kissed and hugged your spouse every day. You probably slept side by side. Losing this kind of physical intimacy can feel devastating.

- Even though you can never replace your partner's special touch, you probably know several people who enjoy hugging or physical touching. If you're comfortable with their touch, encourage it in the weeks and months to come.

- Hug someone you feel safe with. Kiss your children or a friend's baby. Walk arm in arm with a neighbor.

- You might also appreciate massage therapy. Try a session and see how it feels for you.

CARPE DIEM:
Try hugging your close friends and family members today, even if you usually don't. You just might like it!

45.
READ OLD LETTERS

- You may have saved love letters that your spouse wrote to you early in your relationship. These keepsakes are often very intimate and special. They capture those heady, thrilling feelings of new love. They're also a record of your early life together—where you lived, places you went, people you knew.

- Old letters help you remember. And remembering is one of your six central reconciliation needs.

- When you're feeling ready and you have some privacy for a few hours, get out that old box of letters. Immerse yourself in them. Try to hear your spouse's voice speaking the words. Cry, laugh, remember. Reading these special letters may be painful, but I promise you that it will also help you convert your relationship with your spouse from one of presence to one of memory. Reading these letters will help you on your path to healing.

- If you don't have old love letters, get out photos from your dating days instead. Spend some time remembering the early days of your love. Close your eyes and sink back into this time period. Try to conjure up sounds, smells, and tactile memories. For example, when and where was your first kiss? What did it feel like?

· CARPE DIEM:

Decide what you would like done with these letters after you are gone. Do you want your children or other family members or friends to have them? If so, put the letters in a box or an envelope and tape a note to the outside indicating who is to have the letters. If you want the letters to be disposed of after you die, mark the box *Private—to be discarded.*

46.
WRITE A NEW LETTER

- Sometimes articulating our thoughts and feelings in letter-form helps us understand them better.

- Write a letter to your spouse telling him or her how you feel now. Consider the following prompts:
  - What I miss most about you is . . .
  - What I wish I'd said or hadn't said is . . .
  - What I remember best about you is…
  - What's hardest for me now is . . .
  - What I'd like to ask you is . . .
  - I'm keeping my memories of you alive by . . .

- You might consider writing a letter to your spouse shortly after the funeral as well as letters later on—on his or her birthday, the anniversary of the death, etc. That way your letter-writing ritual will be an ongoing release and a way to continue to feel connected to this person who played such an important part in your life.

- After my Aunt Helen died, my Uncle Bob began a ritual of writing her a daily letter, telling her of his thoughts and updating her on what was going on in their family's lives. Today, two years later, he is still writing her a letter every day. He tells me this practice has really helped him adjust to his loss.

- Write a letter to God telling him how you feel about the death.

- Write thank you notes to helpers such as hospice staff, neighbors, doctors, funeral directors, etc.

CARPE DIEM:

Write a letter to someone you love who's still alive telling her why she's so important to you. Such letters become treasured keepsakes.

47.
BE MINDFUL OF ANNIVERSARIES.

- Anniversaries—of the death, life events, birthdays—can be especially hard when you are in grief.

- These are times you may want to plan ahead for. Perhaps you could take a day off work on the anniversary of the death. Maybe on the next birthday of your spouse you could visit the cemetery or scattering site.

- Your wedding anniversary may be a particularly difficult day for you this year and in the years to come. You may want to devote an hour or two of each anniversary to reviewing your wedding photo album and reminiscing. This will help you remember the love you shared and keep your spouse's memory alive.

- Reach out to others on these difficult days. Talk about your feelings with a close friend.

CARPE DIEM:

What's the next anniversary you've been dreading? Make a plan right now for what you will do on that day. Enlist a friend's help so you won't be alone.

48.
TAKE GOOD CARE OF YOURSELF

- Good self-care is nurturing and necessary for mourners, yet it's something many of us completely overlook.

- Try very hard to eat well and get adequate rest. Lay your body down 2-3 times a day for 20-30 minutes, even if you don't sleep. I know—you probably don't care very much about eating well right now, and you may be sleeping poorly. But taking care of yourself is truly one way to fuel healing and to begin to embrace life again.

- Drink at least 5-6 glasses of water each day. Dehydration can compound feelings of fatigue and disorientation.

- Exercise not only provides you with more energy, it can give you focused thinking time. Take a 20-minute walk every day. Or, if that seems too much, a five-minute walk. But don't over-exercise, because your body needs extra rest, as well.

- Now more than ever, you need to allow time for you.

CARPE DIEM:
Are you taking a multi-vitamin? If not, now is probably
a good time to start.

49.
UNDERSTAND THE ROLE OF "LINKING OBJECTS"

- You may be comforted by physical objects associated with the spouse who died. It is not unusual for mourners to save clothing, jewelry, books, locks of hair, and other personal items. You may even want to wear your husband's old sweatshirt or sleep with your wife's robe.

- Such "linking objects" may help you remember your partner and honor the life that was lived. Such objects may help you heal.

- Never think that being attached to these objects is morbid or wrong. It's simply a concrete way for you to stay connected to the memory of your spouse.

- Never hurry into disposing of your spouse's personal belongings. You may want to leave some personal items untouched for months or sometimes years. This is OK as long as the objects offer comfort and don't inhibit healing.

CARPE DIEM:
When and only when you're ready, ask a friend or family member to help you sort through your spouse's personal effects. You might want to ask your children to help. Fill a memory box with significant objects and mementos.

50.
KEEP A JOURNAL

- Journals are an ideal way for some mourners to record thoughts and feelings.

- Remember—your inner thoughts and feelings about the death of your spouse need to be expressed outwardly (which includes writing) if you are to heal.

- Consider jotting down your thoughts and feelings each night before you go to sleep. Your journal entries can be as long or as short as you want. Don't worry about your vocabulary, sentence structure, punctuation, etc. The important thing is to express what's going on inside.

- Here are some questions you might want to answer in your journal:
  - If I could talk to my spouse today, what would I say?
  - If we had had more time together, what would we have done?
  - What did I love most about my spouse?
  - What do I miss most about my spouse?
  - What do I want to do now?

- Or keep a dream journal, instead. Keep a blank book in your nightstand for recording your dreams when you wake up.

- If you're not a writer, consider talking your thoughts and feelings into a tape recorder. Your audio journal might allow you to say things you otherwise might not. And replaying your journal entries in the months and years that follow might help you recognize your progress and growth.

CARPE DIEM:
Stop by your local bookstore and choose a blank book you
like the look and feel of. Visit a park on your way home
and write your first entry.

51.
ORGANIZE A TREE PLANTING

- Trees represent the beauty, vibrancy, and continuity of life.

- A specially planted and located tree can honor your spouse and serves as a perennial memorial.

- You might write a short ceremony for the tree planting. (Or ask another family member to write one.) Consider a personalized metal marker or sign, too.

- For a more private option, plant a tree in your own yard. Consult your local nursery for an appropriate selection. Flowering trees are especially beautiful in the spring. You might also consider a variety of tree that your spouse loved or that reminds you of a place that was special to you and your partner. Flowering shrubs are another lovely option.

CARPE DIEM:
Order a tree for your own yard and plant it in honor of your spouse. You'll probably need someone to help you prepare the hole and place the tree.

52.
PLAN A CEREMONY

- When words are inadequate, have ceremony.

- Ceremony assists in reality, recall, support, expression, transcendence.

- When personalized, the funeral ceremony can be a healing ritual. But ceremonies that take place later on can also be very meaningful.

- The ceremony might center on memories of your spouse, "meaning of life" thoughts and feelings, or affirmation of faith.

- Our culture doesn't always understand the value of ceremony. Don't expect that everyone around you will understand your desire to make use of ritual. However, don't allow their lack of understanding to persuade you to forego ceremonies both at the time of the death and months and years into the future.

CARPE DIEM:
Hold a candle-lighting memory ceremony. Invite a small group of friends. Form a circle around a center candle, with each person holding their own small candle. Have each person light their memory candle and share a special memory of your husband or wife. At the end, play a song or read a poem or prayer in memory of your spouse.

53.
ORGANIZE A MEMORY BOOK

- Assembling a scrapbook that holds treasured photos and mementos of your spouse can be a very healing activity.

- You might consider including a birth certificate, newspaper clippings, locks of hair, old letters—anything that helps capture the life of your precious partner or seems meaningful to you.

- Phone others who loved your spouse and ask them to write a note or contribute photos.

- Other ideas: a memory box, a memory quilt, a personalized website. Find a seamstress who can turn an old shirt or blouse of your spouse's into a stuffed animal. These can make wonderful "linking objects," even for us grown-ups!

CARPE DIEM:
Buy an appropriate scrapbook or keepsake box today. Don't forget to buy the associated materials you'll need, such as photo pages or photo corners, glue, scissors, etc.

54.
CONSIDER WHAT TO DO WITH YOUR WEDDING RINGS

- Many widows struggle emotionally in deciding what to do with the outward symbol of their marriage—the wedding ring. The wedding ring, a tradition for centuries, symbolizes the unending nature of love and marriage.

- Should you still wear a wedding ring when you're a widow or shouldn't you? I don't know what Emily Post has to say about this, but as with most things in grief, there is no "correct" answer. You must simply decide what feels right for you.

- Some widows continue to wear their wedding rings just as they did before the death. Some continue to wear them but move them to the opposite hand. Some wear them on chains around their necks. Still others have the stones removed and reset into a new ring or piece of jewelry.

- You might also choose to no longer wear your rings but save them for your children. For safe long-term storage, a safety deposit box at a bank or a secure vault at home is a good idea.

- If others find fault with your decision about what to do with your wedding rings, pay them no attention. This is your business and yours alone.

CARPE DIEM:
If your wedding ring is set with precious gems, bring it to a local jeweler for a cleaning and check to ensure the stones are secure. Losing the diamond now might feel like a double loss. While you're there, you might discuss with the jeweler the various options for restyling the gems.

55.
SUBSCRIBE TO HEALING

- There are a number of healing magazines for mourners. Most include mourners' stories of loss and renewed hope, poetry, and meaningful artwork.

- One of this author's favorites is *Bereavement*, a bimonthly magazine filled with personal stories of loss and healing, grief education, poetry, etc. At the time of this writing, a one-year subscription within the U.S. costs $32 and can be ordered through www.bereavementmag.com.

- Another option is *Grief Digest*. For information, visit www.griefdigest.com.

- Or, instead of a grief magazine, consider a magazine you've always wanted to read but have never allowed yourself the time to.

- My father and I always shared a love for baseball. Shortly after his death I subscribed to *Sports Illustrated*. As I peruse the pages and read about baseball, tennis and other sports we enjoyed together, I just smile and think of the joy our mutual love of athletics brought us.

CARPE DIEM:
Start a subscription today.

56.
DON'T BE CAUGHT OFF GUARD BY "GRIEFBURSTS"

- Sometimes heightened periods of sadness overwhelm mourners. These times can seem to come of out nowhere and can be frightening and painful.

- Even long after the death, something as simple as a sound, a smell, or a phrase that reminds you of your spouse can bring on a "griefburst."

- Allow yourself to experience griefbursts without shame or self-judgment, no matter where and when they occur. If you would feel more comfortable, retreat to somewhere private when these strong feelings surface.

CARPE DIEM:
Create an action plan for your next griefburst. For example, you might plan to drop whatever you are doing and go for a walk or record thoughts in your journal.

57.
THINK YOUNG

- It is the nature of children to live for the moment and appreciate today. All of us would benefit from a little more childlike wonder.

- Do something childish—blow bubbles, skip rope, visit a toy store, build a sand castle, fly a kite, climb a tree.

- If kids aren't already a part of your life, make arrangements to spend some time with them. Volunteer at a local school. Take a friend's children to the park one afternoon.

- If you and your partner shared your younger years (perhaps you dated in high school or were married as young adults), think back to those times and recall how it felt to be young and in love. This exercise may make you feel sad, but it may also help you feel grateful that you had the privilege of experiencing such a heady, vibrant love.

- What was your favorite activity as a kid? I liked to ride bike and play catch. Plan to give one of your old favorites another try today.

CARPE DIEM:
Buy a gift for a child today just because.

58.
TALK TO YOURSELF ABOUT DATING AGAIN

- You're no longer married. Though you may wish you weren't, you're single. In time, you will need to decide whether you would consider dating again.

- I find that many widows change their minds about this topic over the course of a few years. In the early months after the death, many widows say they won't date and can't imagine themselves ever being with another partner. Later on, they slowly come to understand that the enjoyment of a new love isn't a betrayal of the old one.

- It's OK to waffle about dating and for your feelings about it to change. What's important is that you allow yourself to think through all the possibilities—opposite-sex friendships, simple dating, physical relationships, remarriage—and don't close yourself off to any possibilities. You may have many, many years of life on this earth yet to live. Would it make you happier to share them with someone?

- Your friends and family may encourage you to meet so-and-so or to try such-and-such singles group. Know that they just want you to be happy. If you don't want to date, tell them so.

CARPE DIEM:
You may be concerned about what your spouse would think about your re-entry into the world of dating. Consider that many terminally ill people, acutely aware of life's joys and brevity, encourage their partners to find love again. Write a letter to your spouse in which you discuss your thoughts, fears, and hopes about dating again.

59.
TALK TO YOURSELF ABOUT SEX

- Your sexual partner is gone. If you had a satisfying sexual relationship, it is part of what you lost and is now part of what you grieve. It is normal to miss having sex! Give yourself permission to mourn this aspect of your relationship. If you had a less-than-satisfying sexual relationship, you may grieve the lack or you may regret not working harder on this issue while your spouse was still alive.

- You may also mourn the loss of non-sexual physical intimacy. Your spouse may have been the only person to hug you, to hold your hand, to kiss you, to sleep beside you.

- Consider what you will do about sex in the coming months and years. Just because your partner died doesn't mean your desire has died, too. Be honest and realistic with yourself.

- It may have been many years since you were physically intimate with anyone other than your spouse. Or perhaps your spouse was your "one and only"! Give yourself ample time to think and feel through the possibility of entering a sexual relationship with someone else. Don't proceed until you are absolutely sure and emotionally and physically prepared. Be true to yourself.

- Having sex with someone new is sure to give rise to all sorts of complicated issues and feelings. Your grief may flare anew. If this happens, give yourself adequate time and space to mourn.

CARPE DIEM:

If you haven't had one in a few years, get a complete physical, including a Pap smear and mammogram if you're a woman and a prostate and testicular check if you're a man. If you're of childbearing age and are concerned about pregnancy, talk to your doctor about contraception. It's healthiest to know your body and be prepared.

60.
LISTEN TO THE MUSIC

- Music can be very healing to mourners because it helps us access our feelings, both happy and sad. Music can soothe the spirit and nurture the heart.

- All types of music can be healing—rock & roll, classical, blues, folk.

- Consider listening to music you normally don't, perhaps the opera or the symphony. Or make a recording of your favorite songs, all together on one tape.

- Do you play an instrument or sing? Allow yourself the time to try these activities again soon.

- What music did you and your spouse enjoy listening to together? What was "your song"? At first, hearing your special music may be too painful. But later you may find that playing music that reminds you of your spouse helps you keep her memory alive in your heart.

CARPE DIEM:
Visit a music store today and sample a few CDs or cassettes.
Buy yourself the one that moves you the most.

61.
PRAY

- Prayer is a way of communicating your innermost thoughts and feelings to the powers of the universe. As such, prayer is a form of mourning. And studies have shown that prayer can actually help people heal.

- If you believe in a higher power, pray. Pray for your spouse. Pray for your questions about life and death to be answered. Pray for the strength to embrace your pain and to heal over time. Pray for others affected by this death.

- When you were a child, your parents may have taught you a simple prayer to say at bedtime. Do you remember it? Try adding it to your bedtime routine once again.

- Many places of worship have prayer lists. Call yours and ask that your name be added to the prayer list. On worship day, the whole congregation will pray for you. Often many individuals will pray at home for those on the prayer list, as well.

CARPE DIEM:

Bow your head right now and say a silent prayer. If you are out of practice, don't worry; just let your thoughts flow naturally.

62.
LEARN SOMETHING NEW

- Sometimes mourners feel stuck. We can feel depressed and the daily routine of our lives can be joyless.

- Perhaps you would enjoy learning something new or trying a new hobby.

- What have you always wanted to learn but have never tried? Playing the guitar? Woodworking? Speaking French? Is there something your spouse always wanted to learn to do but never did? Maybe you could learn on her behalf.

- Consider physical activities. Learning to play golf or swimming have the added benefits of exercise.

- Some people like to try a hobby or activity their spouse once enjoyed. This can be a way of giving tribute to your partner and feeling close to her at the same time.

CARPE DIEM:
Get ahold of your local community calendar and sign up for a class in something you have never tried before.

63.
PICTURE THIS

- The visual arts have a way of making us see the world anew.

- Perhaps you would enjoy a visit to an art gallery or museum, a sculpture garden, a photography exhibit.

- Why not try to create some art yourself? Attend a watercolor or calligraphy class.

- Making pottery is something almost everyone enjoys. It's tactile and messy and whimsical. Or you could visit a ceramics shop and simply paint pottery that's already been made.

CARPE DIEM:

Buy some paints, some brushes, and a canvas and paint your feelings about the death. Don't worry about your artistic abilities; just let your imagination take charge.

64.
VOLUNTEER

- Consider honoring your spouse's death through social activism. If she died of heart disease, collect money for the American Heart Association. If he had multiple sclerosis, walk in the annual MS walk nearest you.

- My father died from malignant melanoma (the deadliest form of skin cancer). I help sponsor an annual run/walk in my community that raises money to help combat this horrible disease. The contribution I make every year helps me remember my dad and feel like I'm helping prevent similar deaths in the future.

- Volunteer at a senior center, an elementary school, a local hospital—someplace befitting the memory of your husband or wife.

- If your schedule is too hectic and you can afford it, offer money instead of time. Make your donation in memory of your partner.

- Beware of over-volunteering. Sometimes widows throw themselves into too many volunteer activities in an attempt to "keep busy." Give yourself ample time to mourn.

CARPE DIEM:
Call your local United Way and ask for some suggestions about upcoming events you could participate in.

65.
VISIT THE GREAT OUTDOORS

- For many people it is restorative and energizing to spend time outside.

- Mourners often find nature's timeless beauty healing. The sound of a bird singing or the awesome presence of an old tree can help put things in perspective.

- Go on a nature walk. Or camping. Or canoeing. The farther away from civilization the better. Mother Earth knows more about kicking back than all the stress management experts on the planet—and she charges far less.

- What was your spouse's favorite outdoor get-away? It may be as awesome as a mountain peak or as simple as your own backyard. Wherever it is, go there if you can. Sit in quiet contemplation of your marriage. Offer up your thanks for the love you shared. Close your eyes and feel your spouse's spirit surround you.

CARPE DIEM:
Call your area forest service for a map of nearby walking or hiking trails. Take a hike sometime this week.

66.
SURF THE WEB

- The World Wide Web has a number of interesting and informative resources for mourners.

- Many articles about grief are available online. Books can also be purchased online. Most grief organizations now have Web pages. One online resource is called WidowNet. Its web address is www.widownet.org. AARP also has a great deal of information for widows online. Visit www.aarp.org.

- Search the words "grief" and "widow" and see what you find. You may find a chatroom or message board with helpful stories and support from other widows. Yahoo maintains a number of online support groups for widows. Go to http://groups.yahoo.com and search "widow" to see which groups are currently active and accepting new members.

- Consider setting up your own website and telling your grief story online. You could also use this forum to memorialize your spouse. Personal story websites like these can be poignant and healing both for the poster and the visitor.

CARPE DIEM:
Sit down at your computer today and do a search. If you don't own a computer or have access to one at work, visit your local library. Don't forget to visit the Center for Loss website: www.centerforloss.com.

67.
WATCH FOR WARNING SIGNS

- Sometimes mourners fall back on self-destructive behaviors to get through this difficult time.

- Try to be honest with yourself about drug or alcohol abuse. Any kind of addictive behavior that is ultimately self-destructive can be a "red flag" that you need to get some help with your grief. This might include use of drugs or alcohol, gambling, promiscuous sex, or difficulties in your work and personal relationships. If you're in over your head, ask someone for help.

- Are you having suicidal thoughts and feelings? Are you isolating yourself too much? Talk to someone today. Let people know you are hurting. They can't read your mind or open your heart.

CARPE DIEM:
Acknowledging to ourselves that we have a problem may come too late. If someone suggests that you need help, consider yourself lucky to be so well-loved and get help immediately.

68.
SIMPLIFY YOUR LIFE

- Many of us today are taking stock of what's really important in our lives and trying to discard the rest.

- Mourners are often overwhelmed by all the tasks and commitments we have. If you can rid yourself of some of those extraneous burdens, you'll have more time for mourning and healing.

- What is it that is overburdening you right now? Have your name taken off junk mail lists, ignore your dirty house, stop attending any optional meetings you don't look forward to.

CARPE DIEM:
Cancel your newspaper subscription(s) if you're depressed by what you read. Quit watching TV news for a while.

69.
ESTABLISH A MEMORIAL FUND IN THE NAME OF THE SPOUSE WHO DIED

- Sometimes bereaved families ask that memorial contributions be made to specified charities in the name of the person who died. This practice allows friends and family members to show their support while helping the family feel that something good came of the death.

- You can establish a personalized and ongoing memorial to your spouse.

- What was meaningful to your husband or wife? Did she support a certain nonprofit or participate in a certain recreational activity? Was he politically active or affected by a certain illness?

- Your local bank or funeral home may have ideas about how to go about setting up a memorial fund.

CARPE DIEM:

Call a friend or family member and together brainstorm a list of ideas for a memorial. Suggest that both of you commit to making at least one additional phone call for information before the day is out.

70.
OR CHOOSE TO MEMORIALIZE YOUR SPOUSE IN OTHER SPECIAL WAYS

- Setting up a memorial fund is just one way to honor the life of your spouse. Your family may come up with many other creative ideas.

- Consider your partner's loves and passions. If he were still here, what would make him proud to have his name associated with?

- Some families have set up scholarship funds. Some have donated books to the library or schools. Some have donated park benches or picnic tables, inscribed with an appropriate plaque. Some have planted gardens.

- You might also choose to carry on with something your spouse loved to do or left unfinished.

CARPE DIEM:

Ask yourself: What did my spouse really love in life? What was most important to her? How can I keep this love alive?

71.
PREPARE YOURSELF FOR THE HOLIDAYS

- Because your spouse is no longer there to share the holidays with, you may feel particularly sad and vulnerable during Christmas, Easter, and other holidays.

- You probably remember many of the things your spouse did or said each holiday, and even memories may now feel painful. Over time, you will come to appreciate your holiday memories again.

- Don't overextend yourself during the holidays. Don't feel you have to shop, bake, entertain, send cards, etc. if you're not up for it.

- Sometimes old holiday rituals are comforting after a death and sometimes they're not. Continue them only if they feel good to you; consider creating new ones, as well.

CARPE DIEM:
What's the next major holiday? Make a game plan right now and let those you usually spend the day with know of your plan well in advance.

72.
FIND A GRIEF "BUDDY"

- Though no one else will grieve this death just like you, there are often many others who have had similar experiences. We are rarely totally alone on the path of mourning. Even when there is no guide, there are fellow travelers.

- Find a grief "buddy"—someone who is also mourning the death of a partner, someone you can talk to, someone who also needs a companion in grief right now.

- Make a pact with your grief buddy to call each other whenever one of you needs to talk. Promise to listen without judgment. Commit to spending time together.

- You might arrange to meet once a week for breakfast or lunch with your grief buddy.

CARPE DIEM:
Do you know someone who also needs support after the death of a spouse? Call her and ask her out to lunch today. If it feels right, discuss the possibility of being grief buddies.

73.
BE YOU

- You are a unique individual apart from your relationships with others. Remembering this fact can be a difficult task after the death of a spouse. But you are one single person with singular experiences and thoughts and feelings.

- Now is the time to recall who you are. Who are you, anyway? What are your likes and dislikes? What makes you feel good? What feels "right"?

- Psychologists use the theory of "congruency" to explain why things either feel "right" or "not right." If you are making choices that are congruent—in other words, in alignment with—your true beliefs and values, your choices will feel "right." Are you living a life that is congruent with the real you?

- What gives you joy? Not you and your family, but YOU. This may be the most important question to ask yourself right now.

- If you are choosing to spend your time in ways that don't give you joy, make different choices. You still have to wash the dishes and do your taxes, but in your leisure time and your spiritual time (and even your work time), give up activities that drain you or leave you feeling hollow. Choose activities that fill you up emotionally and spiritually.

CARPE DIEM:

Today, name one ongoing, optional activity in your life that does not give you joy and commit to quitting it. Name one ongoing, joy-giving activity to replace it with and take steps to begin the new activity.

74.
IGNORE HURTFUL ADVICE

- Sometimes well-intended but misinformed friends will hurt you unknowingly with their words.

- You may be told (and you may think in response...):
  - I know how you feel. (Unless you're a widow, you really don't.)
  - _____ would want you to get on with your life. (Maybe so, but he would also understand why I'm so sad.)
  - You'll find someone else. (I can't even begin to think about remarriage yet. And even if I did remarry, it would never replace what I have lost.)
  - Be glad you had her as long as you did. (Of course I'm glad! I'm mourning all the months and years that I won't have her!)
  - If your spouse was sick: It's probably a blessing/for the best. (Even when the death brings some feelings of relief or release, it doesn't necessarily feel like a "blessing.")
  - Time heals all wounds. (Actually, time by itself doesn't heal; mourning does.)
  - It's all part of God's plan. (Then God has pretty crappy planning skills.)

- Don't take this advice to heart. Such clichés are often offered because people don't know what else to say. The problem is, phrases like these diminish your unique and significant loss.

CARPE DIEM:
Consider the clichés you've spoken to mourners in the past in an attempt to comfort them. Forgive yourself just as you should forgive your friends.

75.
MAKE A LIST OF GOALS

- While you should not set a particular time and course for your healing, it may help you to have made other life goals for the coming year.

- Make a list of short-term goals for the next three months. Perhaps some of the goals could have to do with mourning activities (e.g., making a memory book or writing thank-you notes to people who helped at the time of the death).

- Also make a list of long-term goals for the next year. Be both realistic and compassionate with yourself as you consider what's feasible and feels good and what will only add too much stress to your life. Keep in mind that, because of your grief, you may feel more fatigued than usual. Don't overcommit, thereby setting yourself up for failure.

- Try to include at least one or two "just for fun" goals in your list. For example, you might want to take a photography class or learn to tie flyfishing flies.

CARPE DIEM:
Write a list of goals for this week. Your goals may be as simple as:
Go to work every day. Call to make an appointment for a dental
check-up. Take a walk on Tuesday night.

76.
BUT AVOID MAKING ANY MAJOR CHANGES IN YOUR LIFE FOR AT LEAST TWO YEARS

- While it can be helpful to have goals to help you look to a brighter future, it's a mistake to march too boldly ahead.

- Sometimes, in an effort to obliterate the pain and "move forward," widows make rash decisions shortly after the death. Some remarry within months. Some immediately move away from the home they shared with their spouse. Some make bad financial commitments.

- Typically these changes are soon regretted. They often end up compounding feelings of loss and complicating healing as well as creating staggering new headaches. (For example, more than half of all remarriages within the first two years of widowhood end in divorce.)

- If at all possible, avoid making drastic changes for at least two years after the death. You cannot run away from the pain, so don't make things worse by trying to. Instead, give yourself at least a full 24 months to consider whether you should re-marry or relocate or make any other major changes in your life.

- Of course, sometimes you may be forced to make a significant change in your life soon after the death. Financial realities may force you to sell your house, for example. In these cases, know that you are doing what you must and trust that everything will work out.

CARPE DIEM:

If you are tempted to voluntarily make a major change during the first 24 months after the death, force yourself to justify why the change must be made right away. Most of the time, new opportunities can wait two years or longer, or until you're truly ready.

77.
COUNT YOUR BLESSINGS

- You may not be feeling very good about your life right now. You may feel that you are unlucky. You may feel you are destined to be unhappy. You may feel that the universe is conspiring against you. That's OK. There is, indeed, a time for every purpose under heaven—including self-doubt. Indeed, self-doubt is as normal a part of grief as anger or sadness.

- Still, you are blessed. Your life before you met your spouse had purpose and meeting. The life you shared with your spouse had purpose and meaning. And your life now has purpose and meaning, even without the presence of your beloved spouse. It will just take you some time to think and feel this through for yourself.

- Think of all you have to be thankful for. This is not to deny the hurt, for the hurt needs to take precedence right now. But it may help to consider the things that make your life worth living, too.

CARPE DIEM:
If you're feeling ready, make a list of the blessings in your life: your family, your friends, your job, your house. Be specific. "I'm thankful for little Emily's smile. My tea roses. The warm sun on my face."

78.
ASK YOURSELF TWO QUESTIONS: WHAT DO I WANT? WHAT IS WANTED OF ME?

- The answers to these two questions may help you not only survive the coming months and years, but learn to love life again.

- First, now that your spouse is gone, what do you want? What do you want to do with your time? Where do you want to live? With whom do you want to socialize? Whom do you want to be near? These are big questions that may take some time for you to answer.

- Second, what is wanted of you? Who needs you? Who depends upon you? What skills and experience can you bring to others? What are you good at? Why did God put you here on this earth? While considering what you want is important, it alone does not a complete life make.

- Asking yourself these questions on a daily basis may help you focus on the here-and-now. What do I want from my life today? What is wanted of me today? Living in the moment will help you better cope with your grief.

CARPE DIEM:
Write down these two questions on a piece of paper and answer them as carefully and completely as you can.

79.
DO SOMETHING YOU'RE GOOD AT

- Often it helps mourners to affirm their worth to others and to themselves.

- Do something you're good at! Ride a bike. Bake a cake. Do the crossword puzzle. Write a poem. Play with your kids. Talk to a friend.

- Have other people told you you're good at this or that? Next time you're complimented in this way, take it to heart! Embrace your gifts that are God-given.

- What did your spouse most admire about you? Honor his memory by making an effort to keep up with these things.

CARPE DIEM:
Make a list of ten things you're good at. Do one of them today and, afterwards, reflect on how you feel.

80.
IMAGINE YOUR SPOUSE IN HEAVEN

- Do you believe in an afterlife? Do you hope that your spouse still exists in some way?

- Most mourners I've talked to—and that number runs into the tens of thousands—are comforted by a belief or a hope that somehow, somewhere, their loved one lives on in health and happiness. For some, this belief is grounded in religious faith. For others it is simply a spiritual sense.

- If you do believe in an afterlife, you may feel like you can still have a kind of spiritual relationship with your spouse. You may still talk to your wife in the hopes that she can somehow hear you. You may send your husband unspoken messages every night when you go to bed. There is nothing wrong with trying to communicate with your spouse now and always—as long as your focus on this continued relationship doesn't prevent you from interacting with and loving people who are still alive.

- Some widows have dreams in which their partner seems to be communicating back to them. Some feel the overwhelming presence of their husband or wife on occasion. Some actually "see" or "hear" their spouse. These are common, normal experiences and are often quite comforting.

CARPE DIEM:
If you believe in heaven, close your eyes and imagine what it
might be like. Imagine your spouse strong and smiling.
Imagine her waving to you. And imagine your reunion
with her when, one day, you come to join her.

81.
PRACTICE BREATHING IN AND OUT

- After a spouse dies, sometimes what we need most is just to "be." In our goal-oriented society, many of us have lost the knack for simply living.

- Drop all your plans and obligations for today and do nothing.

- Meditate if meditation helps center you. Meditation is simply quiet, relaxed contemplation. You needn't follow any particular rules or techniques. Simply find a quiet place where you can think without distraction and rid your mind of superficial thoughts and concerns. Be still, close your eyes, and focus on breathing in and out. Relax your muscles. Listen to your own heartbeat.

- Many therapists and holistic caregivers recommend breathing exercises to help people relax and live in the moment. Try this one: Imagine that you are breathing in not air but cosmic energy. Feel the energy of the entire universe entering your body each time you inhale. Allow this energy to purify your body, your mind, and your heart. As you exhale, imagine that you are breathing out all your negativity and sadness. Allow your grief, just for the moment, to flow out of you. Give your grief over to a power greater than yourself for a few minutes.

- Yoga is essentially a combination of exercise and meditation. Proper breathing techniques are essential to this age-old practice. Try taking a yoga class and see how you like it.

CARPE DIEM:
While breathing deeply and slowly, try reflecting on this thought:
"As I allow myself to mourn, I create an opening in my heart.
Releasing the tensions of grief, surrendering to the struggle,
means freeing myself to go forward."

82.
TALK OUT LOUD TO YOUR SPOUSE

- Sometimes it feels good to talk to your spouse. Pretend he's sitting in the chair across from you and tell him how you're doing.

- Talk to photos of your beloved partner. Share your deepest thoughts and feelings with her. Make it part of your daily routine to say "Good morning!" to that photo on your nightstand. (Just be careful who's in earshot! Ha-ha!)

- Visit the cemetery (or columbarium or scattering place if your spouse was cremated) and if you're not too self-conscious, talk to your husband or wife.

- Keep symbols of your spouse around, such as photos or personal belongings that help connect you with the spouse who died. They also help activate your need to mourn.

CARPE DIEM:
If you haven't already, put a photo of your spouse in your wallet or purse. Look at it and maybe even talk to it when you're really missing your husband or wife.

83.
DRAW A "GRIEF MAP"

- The death of your spouse may have stirred up all kinds of thoughts and feelings inside you. These thoughts and feelings may seem overwhelming or even "crazy."

- Rest assured that you're not crazy, you're grieving. Your thoughts and feelings—no matter how scary or strange they seem to you—are normal and necessary.

- Sometimes, corralling all your varied thoughts and feelings in one place can make them feel more manageable. You could write about them, but you can also draw them out in diagram form.

- Make a large circle at the center of your map and label it GRIEF. This circle represents your thoughts and feeling since the death. Now draw lines radiating out of this circle and label each line with a thought or feeling that has contributed to your grief. For example, you might write ANGER in a bubble at the end of one line. Next to the word anger, jot down notes about why you feel mad.

- Your grief map needn't look pretty or follow any certain rules. The most important thing is the process of creating it. When you're finished, explain it to someone who cares about you.

CARPE DIEM:
Stop by your local art supply or hobby shop today and pick up a large piece of poster board or banner paper. Set aside an hour or so to work on your grief map today.

84.
TALK TO A COUNSELOR

- While grief counseling is not for everyone, many mourners are helped through their grief journeys by a compassionate counselor. It's not indulgent or crazy to see a counselor after a spouse dies— it's simply good self-care!

- If possible, find a counselor who has experience with grief and loss issues.

- Ask your friends for referrals to a counselor they've been helped by.

- Your religious leader may also be a good person to talk to during this time, but only if she affirms your need to mourn this death and search for meaning.

CARPE DIEM:
Schedule an initial interview with at least two counselors so you can see whom you're most comfortable with.

85.
LOOK INTO SUPPORT GROUPS

- Grief support groups are a healing, safe place for many mourners to express their thoughts and feelings. Sharing similar experiences with other widows may help you feel like you're not alone, that you're not going crazy.

- Support groups give you a time and a place—as well as permission—to mourn. They can also help you assess the relationship you had with your spouse and consider the ways in which the death has changed you. Finally, support groups provide you with ideas and choices for reconciling your grief.

- Your local hospice or funeral home may offer a free or low-cost support group. If you have several friends whose spouses have died, you might also ask them if they would like to get together and talk about their grief journeys.

- If you are newly bereaved, you may not feel ready for a support group. Many mourners are more open to joining a support group six to nine months after the death. Some are ready 18-24 months after the death. Do what feels right for you.

CARPE DIEM:
Call around today for support group information. If you're feeling ready, plan to attend a meeting this week or next.

86.
HELP OTHERS

- Help others! But I'm the one who needs help right now, you may be thinking.

- It's true, you do deserve special compassion and attention right now. But often, people find healing in selflessness.

- Consider volunteering at a nursing home, a homeless shelter, your neighborhood school Do something your spouse would have appreciated.

- If you're well into your grief journey, you may find yourself ready and able to help other mourners by starting a support group or volunteering at a hospice.

- You might even want to plan a trip to my Center for Loss and Life Transition and attend my small group retreat on "Comprehensive Bereavement Skills Training." I'll leave the light on for you! (Call us at (970) 226-6050 and we'll send you a brochure and application.)

CARPE DIEM:
Do something nice for someone else today, maybe
someone who doesn't really deserve it.

87.
SAY NO

- Especially soon after the death of your spouse, you may lack the energy as well as the desire to participate in activities you used to find pleasurable. The fancy term for this is "anhedonia," which is the lack of ability to experience pleasure in things you previously found pleasurable. (Next time someone asks how you're doing, just say, "Oh, I'm feeling a bit anhedonistic today" and watch the response you get!)

- It's OK to say no when you're asked to help with a project or attend a party.

- Write a note to the people who've invited you and explain your feelings. Be sure to thank them for the invitation.

- Realize that you can't keep saying no forever. There will always be that first family reunion, birthday party, holiday dinner, etc. Choose to be proactive with "firsts," and make a plan for confronting them directly. Don't miss out on life's most joyful celebrations.

CARPE DIEM:
Say no to something today. Allow yourself not to feel guilty about it.

88.
TAKE A MINI-VACATION

- Don't have time to take time off? Plan several mini-vacations this month instead.

- What creative ideas can you come up with to renew yourself? Here are a few ideas to get you started.
  - Schedule a massage with a professional massage therapist.
  - Have a spiritual growth weekend. Retreat into nature. Plan some alone time.
  - Go for a drive with no particular destination in mind. Explore the countryside, slow down and observe what you see.
  - Treat yourself to a night in a hotel or bed and breakfast.
  - Visit a museum or a zoo.
  - Go to a yard sale or auction.
  - Go for a bike ride with a friend.
  - Drop by a health food store and walk the aisles.

CARPE DIEM:
Plan a mini-vacation for today. Spend one hour doing something special.

89.
REARRANGE OR REDECORATE YOUR LIVING SPACE TO SUIT YOU

- Marriage is not only a partnership, it is a compromise—a loving compromise, we hope, but still a compromise.

- Each person must make sacrifices for the good of the union. Sometimes these sacrifices are small (such as giving up your habit of leaving your dirty socks all over the house) and some are more significant (such as giving up your career to stay home with small children).

- In a marriage, we make these compromises gladly, knowing we are serving a greater good.

- After your spouse has died, you may find yourself feeling free once again to do what pleases you. This is a normal and often pleasant feeling, and one you shouldn't feel guilty about.

- The house you shared with your spouse is now simply your house. You no longer need to compromise your decorating style or house-keeping habits (unless you live with children, in which case you need to be mindful of their feelings). Recreate your space so it makes you happy.

CARPE DIEM:
What color did you always want to paint one of your rooms but never did because your spouse didn't like it? Stop by the hardware store for a gallon of paint today and paint away.

90.
IF YOU REMARRY, KNOW THAT YOUR GRIEF MUST BE "GRANDFATHERED IN"

- Marrying again feels right for some widows and wrong for others. Neither decision is right and neither is wrong. Simply do what makes you happiest.

- If you choose to remarry, know that you will never get over your grief for the spouse who died. You will always love your previous spouse and, even years and decades later, you will always feel some grief over his or her death. This is normal and necessary.

- Don't make the mistake of thinking that marrying someone else, even someone you truly love very much, will take away your grief. (This is akin to thinking that if your child died, having another baby would quell your grief.) Being with someone you care about may make you less lonely and enrich your life, it's true. But the fact remains: your partner died and you must mourn his death.

- It's important that you let your new spouse-to-be know that your first marriage will always be an important part of your life. It's natural for you to talk about your previous spouse now and then and to continue to display photos of her.

- Of course, carrying a torch that's too bright and too strong may be a sign that you're not ready to remarry. If your grief flickers more than occasionally, you may need more time and space to mourn before you commit to someone else.

CARPE DIEM:
If you're considering remarriage, have a heart-to-heart with your new partner about your grief. Make sure that both of you understand the "grief groundrules" and can support each other's pasts as well as futures.

91.
REMEMBER OTHERS WHO HAD A SPECIAL RELATIONSHIP WITH YOUR SPOUSE

- At times your appropriately inward focus will make you feel alone in your grief. But you're not alone. There are probably many other people who loved and miss your spouse.

- Think about others who were affected by your spouse's death: friends, neighbors, distant relatives, caregivers.

- Is there someone outside of the primary "circle of mourners" who may be struggling with this death? Perhaps you could call her and offer your condolences.

CARPE DIEM:
Today, write and mail a brief supportive note to someone else affected by the death. If you aren't a writer, give them a call or stop in for a visit.

92.
SCHEDULE SOMETHING THAT GIVES YOU PLEASURE EACH AND EVERY DAY

- Often mourners need something to look forward to, a reason to get out of bed today. It's hard to look forward to each day when you know you will be experiencing pain and sadness.

- To counterbalance your normal and necessary mourning, each and every day plan—in advance—something you enjoy.

- Choose something that you like to do—not something you used to do primarily because your spouse enjoyed it. Now is the time for you to begin to consider what makes you happy, what gives you joy. This is not being selfish, by the way. This is attending to your heart and soul.

- Reading, baking, going for a walk, having lunch with a friend, gardening, playing computer games—do whatever brings you enjoyment.

CARPE DIEM:
What's on tap for today? Squeeze in something you enjoy, no matter how hectic your schedule.

93.
TEACH OTHERS ABOUT GRIEF AND MOURNING

- To love is to one day mourn. You have learned this most poignant of life's lessons.

- Maybe you could teach what you are learning to others. Tell your friends and family about the six needs of mourning. Teach them how they can best support you.

- Teach your children about mourning and help them mourn the death of their mother or father. Provide them with mourning opportunities and activities. Model your own grief and mourning openly and honestly. Whatever you do, don't hide your grief in an effort to protect your children. This will teach them to hide their feelings, too.

- Share your wisdom in the safety of a grief support group.

- Remember that each person's grief is unique. Your experiences will not be shared or appreciated by everyone.

CARPE DIEM:
Buy a friend the companion book to this one, called *Healing A Friend's Grieving Heart: 100 Practical Ideas for Helping Someone You Love Through Loss*. It provides concise grief education and practical tips for helping.

94.
SPEND TIME ALONE

- Reaching out to others while we're in mourning is necessary. Mourning is hard work and you can't get through it by yourself.

- Still, you will also need alone time as you work on the six needs of mourning. To slow down and to turn inward, you must sometimes insist on solitude.

- Schedule alone time into each week. Go for a walk in the woods. Lock your bedroom door and read a book. Work in your garden.

- Don't shut your friends and family out altogether, but do heed the call for contemplative silence.

CARPE DIEM:
Schedule one hour of solitude into your day today.

95.
CREATE A SANCTUARY
JUST FOR YOU

• Mourners need safe places they can go when they feel ready to embrace their grief.

• Create a sanctuary in your own home, a retreat that's just for you. Furnish it with a comfy chair, reading materials, a journal, a stereo with appropriate CDs or cassettes. No TV. Or, you may want this to be a room dedicated to silence. As Thomas Moore has noted, "Silence allows many sounds to reach awareness that otherwise would be unheard."

• An outside "room" can be equally effective. Do you have a porch or patio where you can just "be"? Locate a comfortable chair and install a table-top fountain.

• Your sanctuary, even if just a simple room, can become a place dedicated exclusively to the needs of the soul. The death of your spouse requires "soul work." Your creation of a sanctuary honors that reality.

CARPE DIEM:
Identify a spot in your house that can be your sanctuary.
Begin readying it today.

96.
VISIT THE CEMETERY

- Visiting the cemetery is an important mourning ritual. It helps us embrace our loss and remember the person who died.

- Memorial Day, Veteran's Day, Labor Day, Mother's Day, and Father's Day are traditional days to visit the cemetery and pay respects. You might also want to spend time at the gravesite on your wedding anniversary or your spouse's birthday.

- If your spouse's body was cremated, you may want to visit the scattering site or columbarium.

- Ask a friend or family member to go with you. You may feel comforted by their presence. On the other hand, you may find it more meaningful to go by yourself. At times, your aloneness may help you feel closer to your spouse.

CARPE DIEM:
If you can, drop by the cemetery today with a nosegay of fresh flowers. Scatter the petals over the grave. My Uncle Bob always brings fresh flowers to my Aunt Helen's gravesite on her birthday and their wedding anniversary.

97.
GET AWAY FROM IT ALL

- Sometimes it takes a change of scenery to reveal the texture of our lives.

- New people and places help us see our lives from a new vantage point and can assist us in our search for meaning.

- Often, getting away from it all means leaving civilization behind and retreating to nature. But it can also mean temporarily abandoning your environment and spending time in one that's altogether different.

- Visit a foreign country. Go backpacking in the wilderness. Spend a weekend at a monastery. Is there someplace your spouse always dreamed of visiting but never did? Maybe you can travel there on his behalf.

- In the Bible, the career of Abraham begins with God's saying, "Go forth." An alternative translation of the Hebrew is "Go to yourself." The practice of voluntary exile was actually designed to humble oneself and remind oneself that everything comes from God.

CARPE DIEM:
Plan a trip to somewhere far away. Ask
a friend to travel with you.

98.
CHOOSE TO LIVE

- When you got married, chances are you envisioned you and your spouse growing old together and keeping one another company until . . . well, if you're like most of us, you probably didn't picture the until part very clearly.

- "Until death do you part." That infamous and inevitable "until" has arrived, perhaps prematurely (even octogenarians often think of death as premature).

- You didn't have a choice about your spouse's death. You would have chosen for him to live, of course. But you do have a choice about how to spend the rest of your life.

- Will you choose to mourn openly, honestly, and actively so that you can heal? Or will you choose to keep your grief inside and allow it to fester? Will you choose to merely survive? Or will you choose to live?

- I have met thousands of grieving people in my 30 years as a grief counselor and educator. I have seen that those who mourn actively and choose—yes, it's a choice!—to be happy again are happy and go on to live fully the rest of their days.

CARPE DIEM:
Choose to live. You owe it to your children, you owe it to your friends, you owe it to your spouse, you owe it to God, who has given you more precious years on this planet. And you owe it to yourself. Commit today to living.

99.
UNDERSTAND THE CONCEPT OF "RECONCILIATION"

- Sometimes you'll hear about mourners "recovering" from grief. This term is damaging because it implies that grief is an illness that must be cured. It also connotes a return to the way things were before the death.

- Mourners don't recover from grief. We become "reconciled" to it. In other words, we learn to live with it and are forever changed by it.

- This does not mean a life of misery, however. Mourners often not only heal but grow through grief. Our lives can potentially be deeper and more meaningful after the death of someone loved.

- Reconciliation takes time. You may not become truly reconciled to your loss for several years and even then will have "griefbursts" (see Idea 56) forever.

- You'll know that you're beginning to reconcile your grief when it's no longer the first thing you think of each morning. When you start to have some energy again. When you're eating and sleeping well. When you can laugh and have fun once more. When you begin to make plans for the future.

- I believe every human being wants to "mourn well." It is as essential as breathing. Some people make the choice to give momentum to their mourning, while others deny or avoid it. The path you choose to take will make all the difference. Move toward your grief and go on to live until you die!

CARPE DIEM:

Say this to yourself: "I will become reconciled to my grief. If I actively mourn this death, in time my grief will melt into who I am—a happy, loving person who has experienced loss."

100.
BELIEVE IN YOUR CAPACITY TO
HEAL AND GROW THROUGH GRIEF

- In time, you may find that you are growing emotionally and spiritually as a result of your grief journey.

- Growth means a new inner balance with no end points. Your life will never be exactly the same as it was when your spouse was still alive.

- Growth means exploring our assumptions about life. Ultimately, exploring our assumptions about life after the death of someone loved can make those assumptions richer and more life-affirming.

- Growth means utilizing our potentials. The encounter of grief reawakens us to the importance of utilizing our potentials—our capacities to mourn our losses openly and without shame, to be interpersonally effective in our relationships with others, and to continue to discover fulfillment in life, living, and loving.

CARPE DIEM:
Consider the ways in which you may be growing since the
death of your precious husband or wife.

A FINAL WORD

*"If you are seeking a time when you will be finished, you will
never be done."*
    Tibetan saying

As you embrace the precious memories of your spouse, you reconnect
to the meaning and purpose of your life together. As you remember
what you love about your life partner, you welcome him back into
your life even though you are physically apart. You begin to learn to
love him in new and ever-different ways. No, your love does not end
with the death of your spouse.
You can carry him with you into   *You can carry him with you into the*
the future, always remembering   *future, always remembering your past and*
your past and what he brought to *what he brought to the dance of your life.*
the dance of your life.

The journey of grief is never-ending. No, you can never get back to
the beginning of this arduous, life-changing experience, but you do
progress. But to progress requires you to acknowledge your loss and
practice excellent self-care during this time. Remember—it is not selfish or self-indulgent to mourn openly and honestly.

Instead, self-care fortifies you for the ongoing ebbs and flows of your
grief journey, a journey that leaves you profoundly affected and deeply
changed. To be self-nurturing is to have the courage to pay attention
to your needs. Healthy self-
care frees you to mourn in   *Just as you surrendered to the mystery of love,*
ways that help you heal, and   *you must surrender to the mystery of grief.*
that is nurturing indeed.

By taking the vows of love with your spouse, you agreed to share your
life's journey with her, to welcome her as the most important "other"
in your life. Just as you surrendered to the mystery of love, you must
surrender to the mystery of grief. Your commitment to surrender to
your grief is an integral part of your ultimate healing. Then and only

then will you be able to open your heart to live fully until you die. Oh, but once you have the courage and fortitude to do your "work of mourning," your open and grateful heart will fill your soul with love and light!

It is important to me that you know my thoughts and prayers are with you. Yes, it takes patience to discover life again following the death of your beloved spouse. And it takes self-compassion to believe that putting the principles explored in this book into action will actually help the pain of your loss soften over time.

I truly hope that this little book has served and will continue to serve as a loving companion to you. I believe you can and will go on to discover renewed meaning and purpose in your life, in your living and in your loving!

Just one more thing: Right now, take a moment to close your eyes, open your heart and remember the precious smile of your life-partner, your best friend, your lover, and your spouse. As Josh Groban sings in his beautiful song "To Where You Are":

> Fly me up to where you are,
> Beyond the distant star.
> I wish upon tonight
> To see you smile.
> If only for awhile
> To know you're there.
> A breath away's not far
> To where you are.

Thank you for letting me be a small part of your healing. I hope we meet one day.

THE MOURNER'S CODE
Ten Self-Compassionate Principles

Though you should reach out to others as you journey through grief, you should not feel obligated to accept the unhelpful responses you may receive from some people. You are the one who is grieving, and as such, you have certain "rights" no one should try to take away from you.

The following list is intended both to empower you to heal and to decide how others can and cannot help. This is not to discourage you from reaching out to others for help, but rather to assist you in distinguishing useful responses from hurtful ones.

1. You have the right to experience your own unique grief.
No one else will grieve in exactly the same way you do. So, when you turn to others for help, don't allow them to tell you what you should or should not be feeling.

2. You have the right to talk about your grief.
Talking about your grief will help you heal. Seek out others who will allow you to talk as much as you want, as often as you want, about your grief. If at times you don't feel like talking, you also have the right to be silent.

3. You have the right to feel a multitude of emotions.
Confusion, disorientation, fear, guilt, and relief are just a few of the emotions you might feel as part of your grief journey. Others may try to tell you that feeling angry, for example, is wrong. Don't take these judgmental responses to heart. Instead, find listeners who will accept your feelings without condition.

4. You have the right to be tolerant of your physical and emotional limits.
Your feelings of loss and sadness will probably leave you feeling fatigued. Respect what your body and mind are telling you. Get daily rest. Eat balanced meals. And don't allow others to push you into doing things you don't feel ready to do.

5. You have the right to experience "griefbursts."
Sometimes, out of nowhere, a powerful surge of grief may overcome you. This can be frightening, but it is normal and natural. Find someone who understands and will let you talk it out.

6. You have the right to make use of ritual. The funeral ritual does more than acknowledge the death of someone loved. It helps provide you with the support of caring people. More importantly, the funeral is a way for you to mourn. If others tell you the funeral or other healing rituals such as these are silly or unnecessary, don't listen.

7. You have the right to embrace your spirituality.
If faith is a part of your life, express it in ways that seem appropriate to you. Allow yourself to be around people who understand and support your religious beliefs. If you feel angry at God, find someone to talk with who won't be critical of your feelings of hurt and abandonment.

8. You have the right to search for meaning.
You may find yourself asking, "Why did he or she die? Why this way? Why now?" Some of your questions may have answers, but some may not. And watch out for the clichéd responses some people may give you. Comments like, "It was God's will" or "Think of what you still have to be thankful for" are not helpful and you do not have to accept them.

9. You have the right to treasure your memories.
Memories are one of the best legacies that exist after the death of someone loved. You will always remember. Instead of ignoring your memories, find others with whom you can share them.

10. You have the right to move toward your grief and heal.
Reconciling your grief will not happen quickly. Remember, grief is a process, not an event. Be patient and tolerant with yourself and avoid people who are impatient and intolerant with you. Neither you nor those around you must forget that the death of someone loved changes your life forever.

*Helen and Bob Mansfield after
58 years of marriage.
Thanks, Uncle Bob, for your
help in reviewing this book.*

SEND US YOUR IDEAS FOR HEALING A SPOUSE'S GRIEVING HEART!

I'd love to hear your practical ideas for being self-compassionate in grief. I may use them in future editions of this book or in other publications through the Center for Loss. Please jot down your idea and mail it to:

Dr. Alan Wolfelt
The Center for Loss and Life Transition
3735 Broken Bow Rd.
Fort Collins, CO 80526
drwolfelt@centerforloss.com

I look forward to hearing from you!

My idea:

_____

_____

_____

_____

_____

_____

_____

_____

My name and mailing address:

_____

_____

_____

_____

ALSO BY ALAN WOLFELT

UNDERSTANDING YOUR GRIEF
TEN ESSENTIAL TOUCHSTONES FOR FINDING HOPE AND HEALING YOUR HEART

One of North America's leading grief educators, Dr. Alan Wolfelt has written many books about healing in grief. This new book is his most comprehensive, covering the most important lessons that mourners have taught him in his three decades of working with the bereaved.

In compassionate, everyday language, *Understanding Your Grief* explains the important difference between grief and mourning and explores the mourner's need to gently acknowledge the death and embrace the pain of the loss. This important book also reveals the many factors that make each person's grief unique and the myriad of normal thoughts and feelings the mourner might have. Alan's philosophy of finding "companions" in grief versus "treaters" is explored. Dr. Wolfelt also offers suggestions for good self-care.

Throughout, Dr. Wolfelt affirms the readers' rights to be compassionate with themselves, lean on others for help, and trust in their innate ability to heal.

ISBN 978-1-879651-35-7 • 176 pages • softcover • $14.95

Companion
PRESS

All Dr. Wolfelt's publications can be ordered by mail from:
Companion Press
3735 Broken Bow Road • Fort Collins, CO 80526
(970) 226-6050 • Fax 1-800-922-6051
www.centerforloss.com